UNFU YOUR ANGER WORKBOOK

USING SCIENCE TO MANAGE FRUSTRATION, RAGE, AND FORGIVENESS

Dr. Faith G. Harper, LPC-S, ACS, ACN

Microcosm Publishing
Portland, Ore | Cleveland, Ohio

Unfuck Your Anger Workbook: Using Science to Manage Frustration, Rage, and Forgiveness

Dr. Faith G. Harper

All content © Faith G. Harper, 2023

This edition © Microcosm Publishing, 2023

First printing, February 6, 2024

9781648413018

This is Microcosm #557

Cover and book design by Joe Biel

Edited by Elly Blue

These worksheets can be used on their own or as a companion to *Unfuck Your Anger*.

Versions of some of the exercises in this book previously appeared in the *Unfuck Your Anger Workbook* zine, *How to Be Accountable Workbook*, *Unfuck Your Anxiety Workbook*, *Unfuck Your Boundaries Workbook*, and *Unfuck Your Year*.

For a catalog, write or visit:
Microcosm Publishing
2752 N Williams Ave
Portland, OR 97227

(503) 799 - 2698

www.Microcosm.Pub/AngerWorkbook

Did you know that you can buy our books directly from us at sliding scale rates? Support a small, independent publisher and pay less than Amazon's price at www.Microcosm.Pub.

To join the ranks of high-class stores that feature Microcosm titles, talk to your local rep: In the U.S. **COMO** (Atlantic), **ABRAHAM** (Midwest), **IMPRINT** (Pacific), **TURNAROUND** (Europe), **UTP/MANDA** (Canada), **NEW SOUTH** (Australia/New Zealand), **GPG** in Asia, Africa, India, Latin America, and other countries, and **FAIRE** and **EMERALD** in the gift market.

Global labor conditions are bad, and our roots in industrial Cleveland in the '70s and '80s made us appreciate the need to treat workers right. Therefore, our books are MADE IN THE USA.

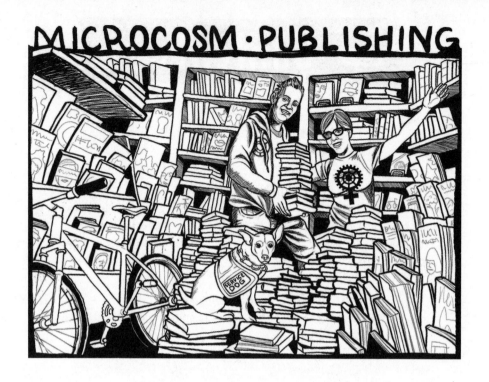

ABOUT THE PUBLISHER

MICROCOSM PUBLISHING is Portland's most diversified publishing house and distributor, with a focus on the colorful, authentic, and empowering. Our books and zines have put your power in your hands since 1996, equipping readers to make positive changes in their lives and in the world around them. Microcosm emphasizes skill-building, showing hidden histories, and fostering creativity through challenging conventional publishing wisdom with books and bookettes about DIY skills, food, bicycling, gender, self-care, and social justice. What was once a distro and record label started by Joe Biel in a drafty bedroom was determined to be *Publishers Weekly*'s fastest-growing publisher of 2022 and #3 in 2023, and is now among the oldest independent publishing houses in Portland, OR, and Cleveland, OH. We are a politically moderate, centrist publisher in a world that has inched to the right for the past 80 years.

Contents

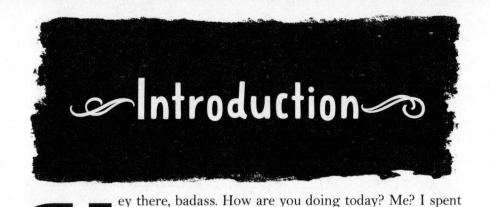
Introduction

Hey there, badass. How are you doing today? Me? I spent hours dealing with replacing a couple tires. And had to walk home in the South Texas heat. And tried to order groceries but couldn't remember how to spell pretzel. Let's just say my frustration level is not that of a blissed out, fully actualized human person right now. So I'm sitting with that. And labeling it for what it is, an AFGO.

Another fucking growth opportunity.

We are all dealing with tons of big, shitty problems that are enough to make anyone angry. People who have hurt us in the past. People hurting us in the present. Incomprehensible levels of political fuckitude. And *then*, as if that isn't tough enough, there are the stupid little things that pile on. Like my day today.

Often, out-of-control anger responses are far more about the little things piling on than the individual event that sets us off . . . so paying attention to *all* of it is how we learn to better manage our anger.

So I started my lunch on the stove. Opened a fancy bottle of root beer. Looked up how to spell pretzel so I could order my groceries and am now having a nice conversation with you.

I did these little things instead of yelling at mechanics and tow truck drivers and anyone who is crossing my path. Or taking out a Costco-sized bag of potato chips. Or anything else of that nature. Instead of being mad at myself for feeling frustrated and upset and un-self-actualized, I'm just feeling what I'm feeling, figuring out what's going on, and working with the very human body-mind I live in.

Being a therapist who understands anger doesn't mean I don't ever get angry. Nor does being in therapy. Nor does being a Buddhist. Or just being someone who continuously works on my shit, as exhausting as it is to do so. Maybe some people transcend . . . but I'm not one of them, and I don't think I'm remotely close to being one of them. But all of those identities have helped me observe my anger differently so that I don't weaponize it into harmful action. And I'm happy with that result. So I'm sharing what I know.

And that's what this workbook is about. If you want to learn more, you can check out my book *Unfuck Your Anger*, but let's give you a little primer on what we're talking about here first.

WHAT IS ANGER?

Anger isn't an on or off emotion. That is, we don't flip a switch from calm to enraged. Anger exists on a continuum. The low end may have us feeling irritated, annoyed, or frustrated; a midpoint of irate, upset, or pissed off; and a boiling point of furious, enraged, or eruptive. Anger is the encompassing term for all of these activating emotional states that are *driving us to action*. Just like every other emotion, what we call "anger" is just our brain's interpretation of our bodies' biochemical reactions.

All emotions are information, designed to help us make decisions that will protect us and keep us safe. They are formed in the middle part of our brain, in our amygdala, based on the information we are processing and our memories of past situations.

The emotions that we think of as positive are a type of "carry on" feedback. These are when our brains are telling us, "Yes! Yes, all cookies! Yes, hiking with friends! Yes, funny movies! These things feel nice, let's do all these things!"

Then there are the emotions that don't feel good, the ones we consider negative. They are the cat scrunched up in the corner, ears flattened and growling, "No! Do not want! Does not feel good or safe or nice at all! Make it stop!" Fear, sadness, jealousy, shame. And, duh, anger. Anger is a huge one, right?

So how does anger work in our brains? When fucked up shit happens, we encode those experiences as *episodic autobiographical memories* or *EAM*. Situations that remind of past fucked up shit activate our survival responses so we don't get hurt again.

Our ability to have a strong response to EAMs is actually a huge evolutionary advantage for humans to a certain extent. The brain remembers the past and presumes it's the future and emotes accordingly (anger, anxiety, fear, etc.) to get us to pay attention. (You can read more about the mechanics of this in my book *Unfuck Your Anger*.)

In modern society, this evolutionary advantage has become a hindrance. The past should absolutely inform our present, but it generally doesn't serve the present. When we were hurt in the past, and it continues to bubble up in the present, it's our primal brain playing the same cassette tape on a loop.

And this emotional state (again, anger, anxiety, fear, etc.) prevents constructive action because it isn't in response to a present threat. Or it just becomes the thing we do because we don't know what else to do with the memories we are living with. EAMs activate an emotional response based on the notion that "it's better to be safe than sorry."

So the short answer? When someone is an immediate threat (real or perceived) to you or someone you love, anger will propel your ability to protect what's important, right?

There's one important caveat here: naturally occuring anger is a survival response not a dominance response. But some people use anger in a willful, conscious way to get what they want. Uncontrolled anger versus manipulative anger can be differentiated by how the angry person reacts when they get their way. If they are still upset after their demands are met, it wasn't a conscious domination tool. If they calm down the minute they are appeased, it was. That's a diagnostic trick that therapists use to see if someone has an anger problem or a coercive control problem (which we talk about in more detail later in this workbook).

HOW TO USE THIS BOOK

When I wrote *Unfuck Your Anger*, I had a lot of worksheets/activity-type things to go with it, to help put into action the mindful work of living with our anger responses. Because everyone is different and needs to unpack their own garbage, right? The problem is it's kinda hard to write all that shit out in a small book. And most people don't want to write all over their books.

So we decided to leave the fundamental questions in the book, but in a list format for people who are discussing or journaling through their process. And *then* create this very workbook-y way for people who want to fill things out in a more structured way. Or copy it off to use over time or more than once. Or with a group. Whatever floats your boat.

This workbook stands alone from the book so you don't have to buy the book for it to make sense. And the book works just fine without the workbook. Nothing chaps my ass more than buying something and being told I have to buy nine more fucking things for it to work. So I won't ever pull that shit on you. You buy (or borrow) whatever of my writings make most sense for you and fuck the rest. It's all good.

You can do any of the exercises in this book in any order. But in our best attempt to be helpful, we did break them down into sections, so if you are focusing on a particular aspect of managing anger, you can access all of those tools in one section. The sections are as follows:

Unpack Your Anger: How we use our anger is what matters. Feeling and acknowledging anger isn't something to be avoided. We don't have to suppress our anger to keep from reacting in harmful ways.

Having a better understanding of anger has the potential to help you in many facets of your life.

In physics there is something called the *observer effect*. This refers to the phenomenon of how simply observing something has an effect on it. The minute you start watching something, the thing that you are watching changes. If you are going to watch some cells on a slide under a microscope, you turn the microscope light on, right? And the cells are going to react to that light.

The same is true of our own emotions. Once we start paying attention to our feelings, thoughts, and physiology we are already starting to make huge changes in how they affect us and how we interact with the world. We are shining a light on our own internal shenanigans. Those big shifts in emotional health start with flipping the light on. The exercises in this chapter do exactly that.

Unfuck Your Anger: We aren't trying to surgically excise anger from our lives. As uncomfortable as it is, it's uncomfortable for a reason. Anger tells you what matters. You will hear that message throughout this book. Which means we need to spend some time figuring out what matters and how we got here. That's this section. Lots of connect-the-dots work so we can see our own patterns up close.

Heal Yourself: So this is the healing part of the program. Activities and ideas that will help you recognize, validate, and respect your anger without letting it run the show in your life.

Heal Your Relationships: Anger doesn't exist in a vacuum, right? Chances are that anger hasn't just hurt you, it's hurt your relationships as well. Pretending otherwise makes for a pretty shitty workbook. So we're not going to. Here are the tools to assist your relationship strengthening, if that's something you are focusing on right now.

Diagnosing Anger: Okay, so when I said you should read whatever sections apply to you and skip the rest? I hope you don't skip this one. Anger itself isn't a mental health disorder, but anger is a key feature in several diagnostic criteria in the Diagnostic and Statistical Manual (which is currently in the text revision of the 5th edition). And we aren't as thoughtful as we could be around this issue—avoiding misdiagnosis, advocating for a correct one (whether as a client or a clinician), and the like. In an era where mental health issues are continuously weaponized, getting things as right as we possibly can is really important. This section also looks at the shadow world of coercive control, as well as ways anger may get turned into self-harm. It's all about understanding underlying etiology so we can support ourselves and our loved ones more skillfully.

So, crack open a root beer, order some pretzels, and start working through this book. Your anger reactions are going to start making a ton of sense really soon. And then you are going to have better tools to manage your responses in a way that's healthy instead of reactive.

Earlier, when I called you a badass? I totally mean that. You've got a great smile, a cute butt, and you are a survivor who has the capability of unlearning your old ways of doing things that helped you survive and learning newer, healthier skills to help you thrive. You got this.

STAY SANE WHILE UNFUCKING YOUR ANGER

I've found over the years that so many people use my books and workbooks to do really difficult unfucking work. This means that even the exercises that may seem fairly straightforward and benign on the surface could end up being pretty intense. Because that's the point, right? Doing hard work in the present in service of a better future.

But that doesn't mean you have to walk around with your entrails hanging out because you are really digging through some emotional muck. These are skills designed to help you stay as regulated as possible while being in the muck. Please consider experimenting with them or finding other regulation skills that work better for you, to help you continue to do something really difficult but valuable.

Ride the Wave

*T*hink of each emotion as a wave crashing on the shore. Different types of waves can represent different emotions. Some days, the surf may be mild and some days it may be huge and stormy. But we don't have to drown in the waves. And we know that we can't stop them from coming. So we surf. I know, easier said than done. When you are having a strong emotional response, try this exercise. Hell, even better...try it now just for practice:

OBSERVE YOUR FEELING

Get curious about what's going on. Notice it and name it.

EXPERIENCE YOUR FEELING

Let the waves come and go. Don't try to block the feeling, push it away, or hold on to it.

DON'T FORGET: YOU ARE NOT YOUR FEELING

Feelings are information. They are something we experience, not something we are. You don't have to act on it. Remind yourself that you have felt different in the past and will feel differently in the future.

DEVELOP AN UNDERSTANDING WITH YOUR FEELING

You don't have to become friends, but you can become more comfortable with its existence. Don't judge it as good or bad, just accept its existence. Maybe you can learn to appreciate what it's trying to tell you.

STOP SKILL

The STOP technique comes from Rob Stahl and Elisha Goldstein's work in Mindfulness Based Stress Reduction (MBSR). It is designed to help us manage stress in day to day interactions, but it is also hugely effective when used during times of intimacy when we find ourselves triggered or activated.

S — Stop. Rather than carrying on as if everything is fine when you are not, stop what you are doing for a moment to check back in with yourself.

T — Take A Breath. Seems intuitive, but it really isn't. When activated, we are far more likely to hold our breath or start breathing rapidly and shallowly. Take a deep breath, with an exhale that is longer than the inhale. This activates the body's parasympathetic system and has an immediate calming effect.

O — Observe. What's going on in your body? Any tension? Numbness? Just notice your somatic reactions instead of trying to disassociate from them.

P — Proceed. Now continue forward, regrounded in the present moment, at a level with which you are comfortable.

TIPP OUT OF CRISIS

Another helpful exercise from DBT is an emotional regulation skill called TIPP, which stands for temperature, intense exercise, paced breathing, progressive muscle relaxation. This is a skill that is completely somatic...meaning body-based. When your mind has hit the overflow point, getting it calm again is most easily accomplished by starting with your body. Rebooting your nervous system then sends the signal to your brain of "ah, ok, I can chill out a little."

T — Temperature: We heat up when we get upset or are in a crisis, and changing your body temperature can signal to your system that it's okay to come down from its extreme state. Splash cold water on your face and wrists, stand in front of the air conditioner, squeeze an ice cube, or eat or drink something cool and see if that helps.

I — Intense Exercise: Release your excess energy, and give your body a sense that you're taking action in response to whatever is upsetting you. Run around the block, do jumping jacks, try a seven minute workout, run up the stairs, do a plank, whatever you can do.

P — Paced Breathing: Take slow, deep breaths to soothe your nervous system and take your nervous system out of fight/flight mode. You can count your breaths, count to five while you breathe in and seven while you breathe out, lie on the floor and do belly breathing, or any other breathing technique that works for you.

P — Paired Muscle Relaxation: This is another way to use your body to signal to your brain that you are safe, and to feel more grounded in your body. One by one, tighten and then relax each part of your body. Make fists with your hands, squeeze, then let them go. Move up your arms, tightening and relaxing, then up through your head, and down all the way to your toes.

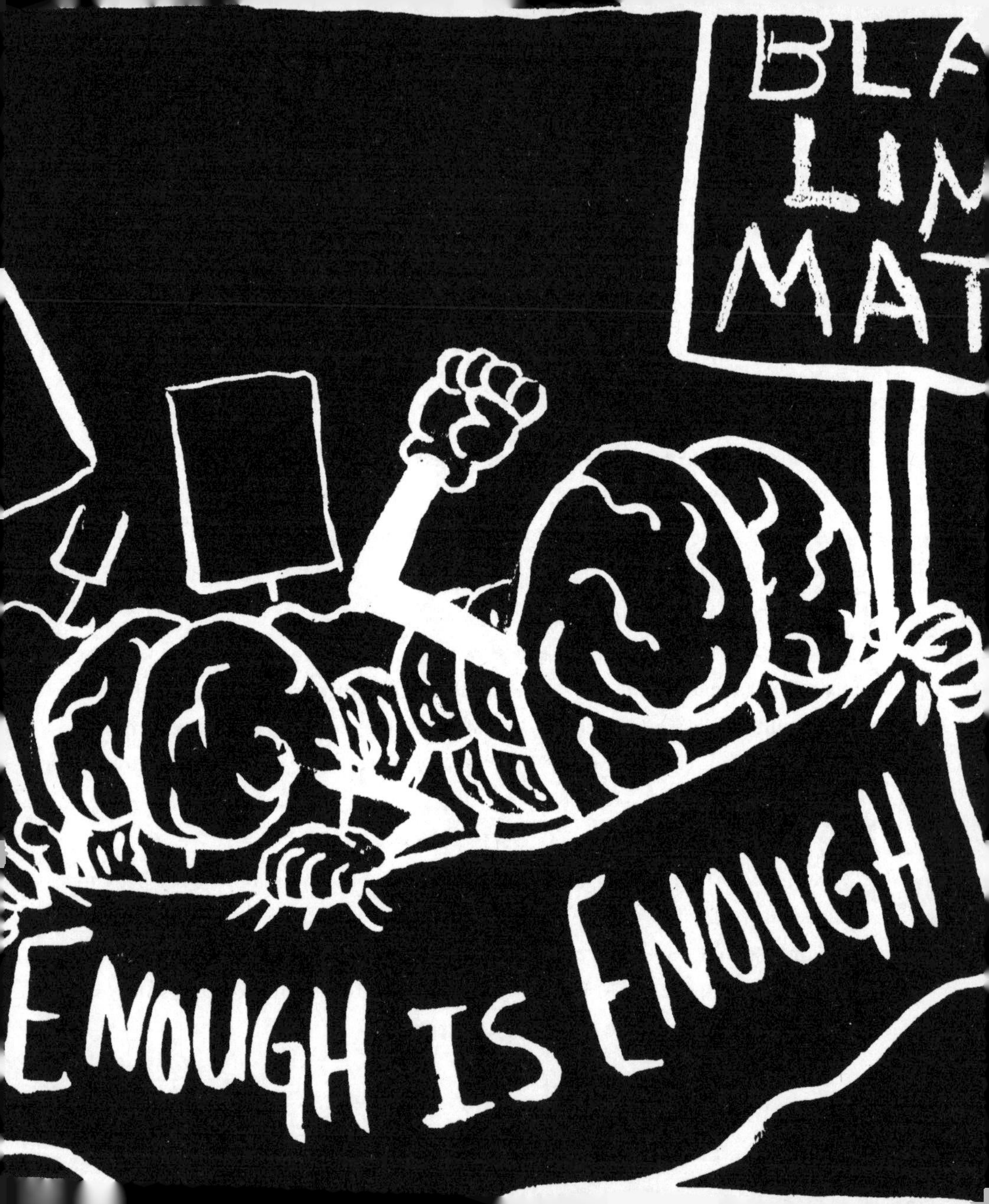
BLA
LIM
MAT
ENOUGH IS ENOUGH

Unpack Your Anger

YOUR ANGER NARRATIVE

We all experience anger in different ways. We are the product of our experiences. What has happened to us, what we have witnessed, what we were taught by others. Being more mindful of our own experiences of anger is the first part in recognizing our own unique experiences of anger. And that allows us a better understanding of them (brain science!) and then managing them (therapy hacks!).

What incident from your past that you have not let go of has the biggest hold on you?

What situations typically trigger anger for you on a day-to-day basis?

What does your anger look like (how do you behave when angry)?

Which of your behaviors fuel your anger and make it worse?

What sensations do you feel in your body when angry?

How does your anger affect your day to day life?

How has anger been destructive to your relationships?

How has it been self-destructive?

Is there anyone in your past that you learned your anger behavior from (anyone you model from or react against?)

In what ways do your anger and pain continue to serve you?

In what ways do they operate as a barrier?

What would life be like if you were not still so angry?

Would working through your anger be worthwhile? How?

ANGER AND OUR UPBRINGING

A huge part of our own healing work is looking at our early experiences around anger. How did we see anger expressed and managed growing up? What did we learn was acceptable? What did we learn was a problem? What did we learn to expect from the people in charge of our safety and care when we were young? These experiences often influence our behaviors in really strong ways, sometimes teaching us what to do, and sometimes moving us to the polar opposite. This worksheet is designed to help you notice your own patterns as you continue your work on managing and expressing anger effectively.

Describe your living circumstances growing up. Did you live with both parents? Other family members? Chosen (non-related) family? Did you have any brothers and sisters? Cousins? Did the circumstances surrounding who you lived with change a lot?

Where did you grow up? Did you move a lot?

What were some of the other close influences in your life? Family you didn't live with, friends of your family, church, clubs, sports involvement?

How was anger expressed in your family while you were growing up? How did your parents/other adult authority figures express anger? The younger members of the household?

Were adults in the household abusive toward each other? Toward you? Toward other younger people in the household? How did you respond in these circumstances?

Were you ever threatened with physical violence (even if it wasn't acted upon)?

How were you disciplined in the home and by whom? How did you respond to this discipline?

How were you disciplined outside the home (school/church/babysitters/scouts/ team sports/etc.)? How did you respond to this discipline?

Did discipline involve physical punishment (for example, being hit with hands, belts, switches, or other objects)? How did you respond to this discipline?

What role did you take in your family? For example, were you the hero, the rescuer, the victim, the clown, the scapegoat, etc.?

What messages did you receive about adult men in your family (father, grandfather, etc.) and men in general?

What messages did you receive about adult women in your family (mother, grandmother, etc.) and women in general?

What messages did you receive about other adults in your family who may be nonbinary or gender-nonconforming?

How were other emotions, such as happiness and sadness, expressed in your family?

Was emotional expression limited to feelings of anger and frustration, or were many different kinds of emotions expressed?

How did adult caretakers respond to your emotions? Were you believed, validated, shut down, teased, etc.? How do you remember responding?

What feelings, thoughts, and behaviors carry over into your relationships today? What purpose do these behaviors serve today? What might change if you changed any of these behaviors?

THE FOUR ANGER CUES

A helpful way of recognizing your anger responses is by noticing your personal anger cues. But it's not quite enough to say "recognize your anger cues," right?

What the fuck do I mean by that? Cues, in this case, are our warning signs that you are becoming or have become angry and it's time to pay attention before you lose your ability to manage it proactively. There are four categories of cues:

Physical Cues: This is how your body responds, like elevated heart rate, breathing, feeling flushed, having your chest get tight or your stomach go all wonky.

What are your physical anger cues?

Emotional Cues: These are the emotions/feelings that often present themselves with anger. Things like hurt, fear, jealousy, etc.

What are your emotional anger cues?

Cognitive Cues: These are the thoughts that you have in response to anger. This could be negative dialogue about the situation, the other people involved, or even yourself. This may also include intrusive images of past issues or aggressive ways you could manage the present situation.

What are your cognitive anger cues?

Behavioral Cues: This is what you actually do with your body, like raise your voice, stomp around, clench your fists, etc.

What are your behavioral anger cues?

Your Personal Cue Profile:

What cues are most common for you?

Did anything surprise you upon reflection?

What do you think you need to be most aware of moving forward?

THE ANGER AROUSAL CYCLE

Now that we have talked about what activates our anger, let's look at how it works inside our bodies. This ties directly to the anger cues exercise because both help you recognize where you are much earlier, giving you more opportunity to respond skillfully. Researchers refer to this as the anger arousal cycle.

The anger arousal cycle has five phases: activation, escalation, crisis, recovery, and post-crisis slump. This worksheet helps you find patterns in your own phase responses. Paying attention to this cycle is incredibly helpful in understanding our reactions and the reactions of others so we can be more skillful in how we approach these issues.

> **Activation:** This is where an event, thought, feeling, or somatic sensation is perceived as a threat to ourselves or someone or something that is important to us. Our physiology activates in order to meet that threat.

> **Escalation:** This is where our activation ramps up and we can really feel the difference in our bodies. Our breathing gets faster, our heart rate and blood pressure go up, our muscles get tense, our voice changes, our eyes and brows change, etc.

> **Crisis:** This is where our physiology takes over, and our vagal tone changes. Meaning we move into fight/flight/freeze response. Our body is looking to take action to defend us and create a mechanism to escape or manage the pain of attack. Once we are in this phase, our executive functioning (thinking brain) stops working as well because we are in survival mode. We act from this phase.

> **Recovery:** This is the phase where our bodies start to return to normal, and our survival mode responses have deactivated. Our prefrontal cortex starts to come back online along with our executive functioning. And while the cortisol takes up to 48 hours to dissipate, the adrenaline starts to leave our body (and some people feel a little nauseated as that happens).

> **Post-Crisis Slump:** To regain balance, the body requires our heart rate to slow below normal for a bit. This, paired with our awareness of our behavior, can lead to regret, guilt, and even depression.

Describe an incident where you were really angry

Now describe what you noticed in your body and mind during each phase of your anger cycle:

Activation

Escalation

Crisis

Recovery

Post-Crisis Slump

FIGURING OUT YOUR LIFEMORTS

LIFEMORTS are the nine rage circuits in our brain identified by neuroscientist and fancy National Institute for Health researcher R. Douglas Fields. Short explanation? There are certain categories of situations that we have adapted an evolutionary response to keep us safe and alive. And anger is an activating response to help us with that staying-alive thing.

This worksheet helps you recognize your emotional labels around anger, the effect they have on your thinking patterns and physical reactions, AND gives you space to recognize your LIFEMORTS triggers. So if you have certain triggers that are particularly apparent, you can plan to deal with them more proactively, right?

Life or Limb: This is where the brain perceives a situation as a literal life-or-death attack and responds defensively.

Insult: This is where the brain perceives an emotional attack rather than a physical one, like a dominance challenge. Dr. Fields calls it the human version of head-butting.

Family: This is where the brain perceives an attack on someone we love, our family as self-defined.

Environment: This is where the brain perceives an attack on our territory, our physical space (home, car, etc.)

Mate: This is where our brain perceives an attack against our romantic partner.

Order in Society: This is where the brain perceives an attack to our place in society. This can be a social justice fueled anger, but is also what often causes mob violence at protests.

Resources: This is where the brain perceives an attack on our resources, like money or possessions.

Tribe: This is where the brain perceives an attack on our identified community, whether our extended family, group of friends, neighbhood, etc.

Stopped: This is where the brain perceives that we are being inprisoned or our progress is being held up by someone else in some way.

ANGRY EMOTION FELT (Irritation, Frustration, Rage, etc)	ASSOCIATED THOUGHTS	ASSOCIATED BODY SENSATIONS	LIFEMORTS TRIGGERS

PERSONALIZING YOUR ANGER EXPERIENCES WITH AHEN

This worksheet is another way for you to observe your underlying patterns related to your experiences of anger. Recall a recent situation where you were angry, and answer these questions about it.

Anger emerges from:
* *Hurt*
* *Expectations not met*
* *Needs not met*

What are the underlying roots of your anger? If you aren't sure, reflect on when you first noticed that you were angry. What was going on around you...sights, smells, noises, people? What were you doing? What were others doing? What were you thinking about? Any particular memories coming up at that time?

Once you figured out these underlying roots, were they legit or were they more about you and your history than about the present situation?

If the roots are legit, are they something that need to be addressed or is it one of those bullshit daily life things that just happens? Speeding ticket, fucked up drive thru order, etc.?

If it needs to be addressed what is the best way to do so? How do you correct the situation with as little disruption as possible?

What can you do to keep from getting further hurt in the process (physically, emotionally, and mentally)?

Can you keep the hurt to others minimal (physically, mentally, and emotionally)?

Does it need to be addressed immediately, or can it wait until you are calmer and feel safer?

Is there anyone you can talk to that is going to have a healthy, supportive perspective...a counselor, friend, mentor, family member? Someone who knows you, loves you, and will totally call you out on your shit if need be.

After you act (instead of react), then evaluate the results. Did it work? Is this a strategy that you can use again? Are you still angry or are you feeling better and safer now?

AHEN IN PRACTICE

Now that you've learned about the root of your anger, notice when you are angry and figure out which HENs are creating that anger.

Situation: My spouse didn't do the dishes.

◯ Hurt

● Expectations not met

◯ Needs not met

Specifics of the underlying HEN: I wasn't hurt and it wasn't a real need, but I had expected to just get started with cooking and felt disappointed and inconvenienced.

Situation:

◯ Hurt

◯ Expectations not met

◯ Needs not met

Specifics of the underlying HEN:

Situation:

◯ Hurt

◯ Expectations not met

◯ Needs not met

Specifics of the underlying HEN:

Situation:

○ Hurt

○ Expectations not met

○ Needs not met

Specifics of the underlying HEN:

Situation:

○ Hurt

○ Expectations not met

○ Needs not met

Specifics of the underlying HEN:

Situation:

○ Hurt

○ Expectations not met

○ Needs not met

Specifics of the underlying HEN:

WHAT AM I FEELING?

I know, I know. You're all kinds of pissed off and are supposed to stop and fill out a worksheet? Fuck off with that. If you can, that's brilliant. But this is also a very helpful tool to use in reflection, after you've calmed down enough to not wad up this worksheet and throw it across the room or something.

1. What am I feeling?

2. What activated me feeling this way? Any LIFEMORTS and AHENs to take into account?

3. What COULD I do about my feeling? What are my options?

4. What AM I going to do about my feeling? What is my action plan?

Unfuck Your Anger

HOW WE HANDLE ANGER

*T*here are multiple ways we can handle our feelings of anger, some of which are generally helpful and others that are far more toxic to ourselves and those around us . . . and the differences can be really fucking subtle. Not to mention they can be circumstance-dependent. How you are with your family may be very different from how you are at work, right?

• **Stuffing** – Anger is swallowed and ignored rather than expressed because it is deemed bad, wrong, or inappropriate.

• **Overt Hostility** – This is open antagonistic behavior used in defense of oneself, regardless of the consequence to others. It could include physical violence or verbal antagonism.

• **Covert Hostility** – While not openly hostile, passive-aggressive people look for means to control situations without expressing their true emotions in an open and vulnerable way. Instead, they will manipulate others in subtle ways. Covertly hostile people are masters at mind games.

• **Boundary Holding** – This means expressing what is okay and not okay without disconnecting from others altogether. It requires a level of vulnerability because it means expressing yourself honestly, knowing that the answer may be no.

• **Releasing** – Dropping anger means recognizing that there are forces outside of your control and that your anger does not serve you.

Reactive	Proactive
Stuffing	*Releasing*
Overt Hostility	*Boundary Holding*
Covert Hostility	

The first three—stuffing, overt, and covert hostility—are reactive, meaning we are operating from a place of being uncomfortable with or overwhelmed by our feelings of anger so we lash out or lash in. This is where most of us operate from. These are the cultural norms . . . the ways of managing anger that we learn from those around us. This habit of not paying attention to what our body is telling us is what causes so many other mental health issues.

The last two—boundary holding and releasing—are practical and proactive means of handling anger. You are not ignoring your amygdala; you are acknowledging the information it is giving you to keep you safe and figuring out what the best course of action is around that information. Is there something you need to act on or is this old stuff coming up?

Holding a boundary means to be assertive rather than aggressive, doing something proactive about the situation that caused your anger response.

Releasing as a means of handling anger is very different from stuffing because you are not trying to pretend the anger isn't there but, instead, are doing the work around detoxing your anger. Releasing is an informed practice of realizing that your anger is directed at something about a behavior that you cannot change or a boundary that you cannot enforce. Releasing often requires forgiveness work—when our anger and resentment have become a long-standing, unresolvable emotional pattern within ourselves (more on that in the Heal Your Relationships chapter).

All of the exercises in this book are focused on the last two means of handling anger. Because we are going to be emotionally mature badasses who don't let anger control everything for the rest of our lives, right?

For each entry, indicate if this behavior is part of your family history or something others have used towards or around you, if you yourself have used this method to handle your anger in the past, or if you currently use this method, and then reflect a bit on the circumstances.

Stuffing

○ *Others* | ○ *Past* | ○ *Current*

In what situations have I used this method to handle my anger?

_____

What other strategies might I use in the future?

_____

_____

Overt Hostility

○ *Others* | ○ *Past* | ○ *Current*

In what situations have I used this method to handle my anger?

_____

_____

What other strategies might I use in the future?

_____

_____

Covert Hostility

○ *Others* | ○ *Past* | ○ *Current*

In what situations have I used this method to handle my anger?

_____

_____

What other strategies might I use in the future?

_____

_____

Boundary Holding

○ *Others* | ○ *Past* | ○ *Current*

In what situations have I used this method to handle my anger?

_____

_____

How can I continue to use this strategy in the future?

_____

_____

Releasing

○ *Others* | ○ *Past* | ○ *Current*

In what situations have I used this method to handle my anger?

_____

_____

How can I continue to use this strategy in the future?

_____

_____

THE CONTINUOUS YOU

This is a super-simple version of a classic exercise from Acceptance and Commitment Therapy. It works well for all kinds of strong feelings. I'm including it here because anger is near the top of the list of emotions that are considered something we "are" instead of something we "have."

This week when you find yourself feeling angry (or even the more mild forms of anger like frustration or irritability), try the following:

Notice what you're feeling. Give the emotion a label (agitated, pissed off, livid).

Now remind yourself that you are noticing this feeling.

And if you are noticing it, it means it's something that you are experiencing, not something that you are.

Remind yourself that what you are noticing changes frequently throughout the week, but the you who is doing the noticing remains the same. Which means your moods do not define you, right?

What did you notice frequently through this week?

What feelings words are attached to that?

How have your feelings changed for noticing them?

SOMETHING PISSED YOU OFF? LET'S SOLVE YOUR PROBLEM

*T*his tool (adapted from *Dr. Weisinger's Anger Workout Book*) is an even more structured way of mapping out and creating solutions. It helps get your thinking brain back online when your emotional (angry) brain is trying to take over the show.

State Your Problem: Identify and define the problematic situation.

Outline Your Response: After describing the details of your problem as specifically and expansively as you can, then detail your usual response. Researchers who studied expert problem solvers found that they didn't look at the problems in abstract terms, but instead focused very concretely on the "who, what, where, when, why, and how" facts.

List Your Alternatives: Brainstorm all your possible solutions. Yes, even "magical thinking" type solutions or "go back to bed and let it figure itself out" solutions. They bubble up, and that's ok. Don't worry about quality, the important thing is quantity. Come up with as many different possibilities as possible.

Visualize Your Consequences: Consider the possible outcomes of all of the alternatives you listed. What might happen in both the short and long term? Are these consequences you can deal with? Cross out anything that is clearly a non-starter. Consider combining alternatives and visualizing how that would work.

Evaluate Your Results: Now you gotta act. Use the same strategy in more than one scenario (you know, on multiple occasions when people piss you off). What are the actual consequences? Is this an improvement over the old ways you responded? Do you need to go back to the drawing board, or do you have a good handle on things now?

IRRITATION   FRUSTRATION   MAD   FURIOUS EXPLOSIVE RAGE

THE "MILK" DEFUSION TRAINING

While everything we feel is real, our feelings don't always reflect reality. We can recognize something as unhelpful to a particular situation but still find it an incredibly sticky internal experience that gets in the way of handling things the way we set out to. This technique is designed to distance you from the stickiness.

Edward Titchener was an English psychologist who developed the idea of structuralism in the field, meaning he was interested in the structure of the mind as a mechanism for emotional healing. This led to a bit of a hack that is used to this day, particularly in Acceptance and Commitment Therapy, as a means of reducing the emotional impact, discomfort, and even believability of our own thought processes.

He found that we render certain thoughts meaningless by fully leaning in rather than ignoring and suppressing. You'll want to be somewhere that people aren't going to think you're a total psychopath, because you are going to have to talk to yourself in your out-loud voice. So maybe save this exercise for when you aren't at the gym or on the bus, okay?

1. Start with the word milk. You're going to repeat it over and over, out loud (yes, it has to be) for 45 seconds. You know, literally just "milk milk milk . . ."

2. Notice how the word started out as something that symbolized some kind of meaning for you. In my case, the word milk is a negative one because I'm allergic to all forms of dairy. But by repeating it out loud it just becomes . . . noise. And doesn't have the same negative connotation anymore.

3. Now take the thought that most activates your anger responses—it can be a word, phrase, or sentence—and do the same exercise. It could be "my mother" or "no one is listening to me at work" or anything that you catch yourself contending with on the regular.

4. Notice what happens to the thought, once you turn it into nonsense sounds. The idea is to inactivate your anger response by defanging the thoughts that help it along. By turning it into nonsense noises, you are creating space between thought and response, either an external behavior or an internal emotional spiral. It happens by disconnecting (defusing) the thought from the meaning you have assigned to it.

What word or phrase did you choose?

What was the immediate effect of repeating it?

What about over time?

WHAT ABOUT WHEN YOU DIDN'T?

Let's look at the times that you didn't manage anger badly. Sometimes the best tools for anger management already lie within you; we just need to figure out how you draw upon those tools on the regular. In therapy-speak, we call these exception-seeking questions

Can you think of a time where you were angry and you didn't let it take you over?

How did you do it?

What was different?

What helped?

RECOGNIZING CONTROL

Humans have a tendency to remember negative things over positive ones. It helps keep us safe, generally, but isn't useful when we are trying to remember the things we've gotten right over the years. We may *see ourselves* as constantly out of control but may have done some solid work that we can build upon by paying attention. This is a journaling exercise based on components of both Acceptance and Commitment Therapy and Solution-Focused Brief Therapy that helps us recognize our capabilities when we feel overwhelmed and out of control.

What if your anger fully controlled you? If you had no capacity for self-management? What would your life be like? Would you even be alive?

What about times when your anger did not control you? Or didn't control you entirely? What did you do? How did you make that happen? What was going on that helped support you being skillful instead of reactive?

HOW CAN YOU REFRAME YOUR EXPERIENCE?

One of the places in which we get stuck is when we frame the story through the lens of how we were the victims of the violence or neglect of others. While those feelings are valid, they impede recovery. Rewriting our story as one in which we survived can dramatically reframe our experience without letting anyone off the hook for the harm they have caused. Once we realize our capacity to survive, we can then focus on our future goals instead of being stuck in the past. Try re-narrating your experience, placing yourself as the survivor instead of the victim:

_____

_____

_____

_____

_____

_____

_____

_____

_____

_____

_____

_____

_____

_____

_____

_____

_____

_____

_____

_____

_____

_____

_____

_____

_____

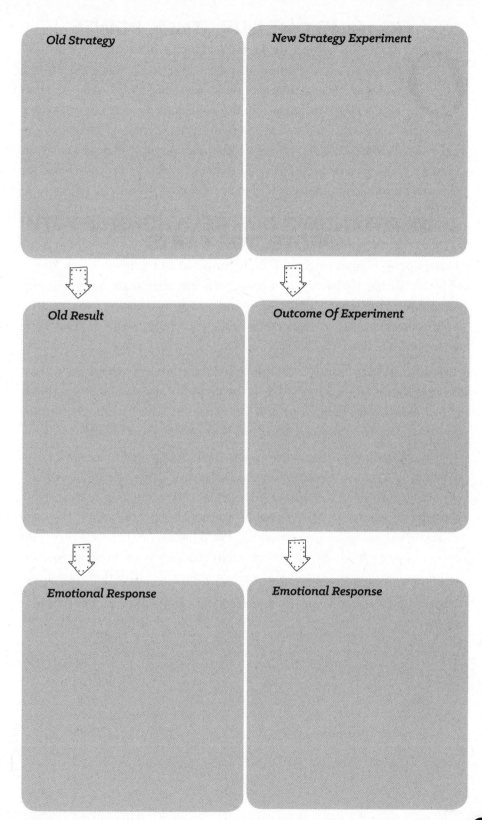

Old Strategy

New Strategy Experiment

Old Result

Outcome Of Experiment

Emotional Response

Emotional Response

47

FIGURING OUT OUR STUCK POINTS

One of the biggest obstacles to forgiveness is our human tendency to keep reacting to hurt in the same ways, despite the fact that these strategies don't serve us. "Well, stop it" is an easy enough response, but human brains do so adore well-worn grooves of behavior…and we have to recognize the grooves before we can apply thde brakes. This worksheet is designed to help you figure out your strategy stuck points by building conscious awareness of your behavior patterns so you can implement a plan for different ways of reacting.

UNDERSTANDING OUR RELATIONSHIP WITH PROTECTOR PARTS

This exercise is from Internal Family Systems, a therapy program founded by Dr. Richard Schwartz that conceptualizes all humans as having sub-personalities (or parts). This may sound a little like having a dissociative identity disorder, but it is more like code-switching, which is something most everyone does.

Code-switching is how we adjust how we present ourselves to best manage the situation we are in. Like being polite and patient when trying to help a child, but being loud and fun when out with friends. Or the customer service voice at work. Everyone has one of those, right?

Code-switching in this sense is when we bring up the aspect of our personality we most need for survival or peace. When working with anger, it may be helpful to think of yourself as code-switching to the part of you that is protective of the rest of you and/or protective of who and what you value and love. You may very well have more than one protector part, and you may find it helpful to identify as many of them as possible and to understand the nuances of each of their roles with these questions.

Start by listening in quietly and focusing on the part of you that gets angry.

What is the intent of that part of you? How is it trying to serve you and/or those you love?

How does that part use anger to "do its job"? In what ways does it help you manage your life?

How does it protect you?

What is it working to protect you from?

How does this part relate to others in your life?

How does it relate to people you love?

How does it relate to people you dislike?

How does it relate to people to whom you have no strong emotional attachment?

How does this part of you feel about its job?

Would it rather be doing something else?

After working with that part of you and these questions, what do you notice about that part? What about your relationship with it?

FIRE DRILL EXERCISE

When we are struggling with anger, we may be struggling against our protector part. And it's pretty hard to face the aspect of ourselves whose job is to fight back, right? This exercise helps the protector part recognize that you are working to stay safe without losing emotional control. That you want to face these issues from a place of a more holistic self.

This exercise is also commonly used in Internal Family Systems. It is referred to as a "fire drill" exercise by IFS creator Dr. Richard Schwartz because protector parts often act as firefighters on our behalf.

Here's how it works:

- Focus on someone in your life (either past or present) who activates anger inside you, but imagine putting them in a room where they cannot leave.

- Imagine yourself watching them through a one-way mirror. They can't see you or hear you or get to you.

- Now imagine them doing or saying the things that upset you, anger you, cause you pain.

- Now notice what happens in your body when your protector part's attention has been gained. Notice how your thoughts change, your feelings change. Notice how your body changes. Maybe you clench your muscles. Maybe your breathing and heart rate go up. Maybe your stomach gets upset. Notice all the ways the protector part changes your body.

- Watch the person in the room with your protector part. What does the protector see in them? What about them makes the protector so determined to keep you safe?

- Now turn to your protector part and reassure it. Let it know you are not entering the room and are not in danger. Encourage the protector part to stand down from its fight.

- Encourage your protector part to release the energy it had gathered on behalf of fighting for you. Don't try to force anything. Just see if the part is able to do so with your gentle encouragement.

- Now check in on yourself. What's going on in your body now? Any changes to how you are holding yourself? Any changes in your breathing and heart rate? What about your thoughts and feelings?

- Now focus back on the person in the room. How do they look to you now?

- Without going into the room (because we promised the protector part!), think about how it would feel to go in as your full self leading the way rather than the protector part?

- Ask the protector part if it can trust you to manage these situations with your full self. If not, what are the reservations the protector part has? What do you need to work on?

- When you're ready to close out this practice, thank the protector part for its support in keeping you safe. And thank them for working with you on trusting you to lead these situations from your whole self.

Once you're done with this exercise, take some time to reflect on how it felt and what you learned.

BIAS DISRUPTORS

The brain has multiple shortcuts it takes to make decisions more quickly and to preserve energy. These shortcuts often serve us well, but when they fail we can get stuck in unhelpful thinking (and subsequent behavior) patterns. Look at how three biases might be affecting your interactions, especially when they activate frustration and anger within you.

For each bias, write down an example of a time you fell prey to it and how you felt under its sway.

Availability Bias: Our likelihood of believing something just because the idea is readily available. Like when several media outlets report that a celebrity died even though that hadn't been announced by anyone who actually knows them, so we believe, understandably, that they are dead. Because five different websites said so and it's trending on TikTok!

Confirmation Bias: When we seek out data that supports what we already believe. If you believe that butter is bad for you, you can easily do a Google search for "butter is bad for me" and find lots of people agreeing that it is. Versus searching for "health benefits of butter" and getting a more even perspective.

Hindsight Bias: When we think we are better at predicting the future than we are, by deciding we "saw something coming" when we actually didn't. We don't like to be surprised and definitely hate being screwed over by someone we trusted. So we may think or say, "I knew they were shady, I just didn't have proof yet!" so we don't feel like we were stupid for not noticing.

INTENTION SETTING

Most of us are used to the idea of goal setting. Goals are about specific, measurable, and quantifiable outcomes. And goal setting is important, so I am not suggesting that you give that up. But . . . in day-to-day life there are many things that are out of our control that can affect our goal attainment (COVID-19, anyone?).

Intention setting is about how we focus our energy on a day-to-day basis. It's about what we set our minds to notice. If you are looking to purchase a new bike, you are going to notice the bikes around you in a completely different way, right?

In this case, if we are looking at ways anger is impacting our daily lives in ways that are causing harm to others and ourselves, intention setting may help remind you of the skills you are building around having more equanimity in your life.

Intention setting is a precursor to goal setting. Intentions are about how we want to interact in the world, what we want to notice, and who we want to be. You can consciously pay attention to opportunities to advance your goals but successful humaning stands apart (and above) our goal achievement. So let's start with our locus of control.

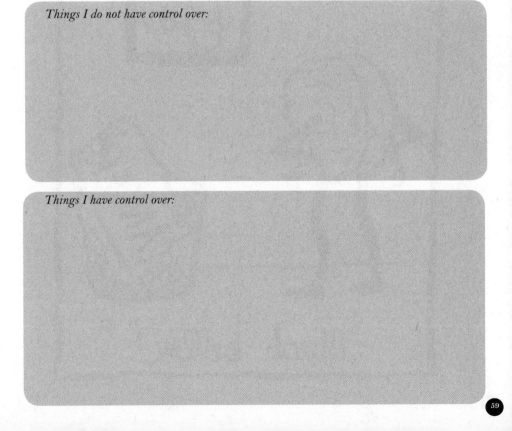

Things I do not have control over:

Things I have control over:

In some way shape or form, your answers centered on the fact that you do not have control over the behaviors of others, but you do have control over yourself right? This is important for intention setting, because whatever you set needs to be grounded in your own locus of control. While "I don't want to argue with anyone" is a nice goal to have, you don't have control over their argumentative nature of someone else. An intention of "I will presume the best intent of those around me" will go a long way to prevent you from starting an argument and will go a long way in helping you manage an argument that you get invited to participate in by someone else, right?

My intention for the week:

A Week of Intentionality

	Sunday	Monday	Tuesday	Wednesday	Thursday	Friday	Saturday
Progress							
Struggles							
What I noticed							

My overall wins: In which ways was I successful with my intention?

My overall growth opportunities: Where did I most struggle?

Is this an intention that is of benefit to me? Do I want to carry it forward or make any adjustments?

MEDITATION ON THE SOLES OF THE FEET

Adapted from a study by Singh, Lancioni, Singh, Winton, Sabaawi, Wahler & Singh (2007)

This may be a "well, duh" thing to say but the more calm and relaxing the atmosphere, the better. Even if you can just dim the lighting a bit it can really help.

1. If you are standing, stand in a natural—rather than an aggressive—posture.

2. If you are sitting, sit comfortably with the soles of your feet flat on the floor.

3. Breathe naturally and do nothing.

4. Cast your mind back to an incident that made you very angry. Stay with the anger.

5. You are feeling angry, and angry thoughts are flowing through your mind. Let them flow naturally, without restriction. Stay with the anger. Your body may show signs of anger (e.g., rapid breathing).

6. Now, shift all your attention to the soles of your feet.

7. Slowly, move your toes, feel your shoes covering your feet, feel the texture of your socks or hose, the curve of your arch, and the heels of your feet against the back of your shoes. If you do not have shoes on, feel the floor or carpet with the soles of your feet. Keep breathing naturally and focus on the soles of your feet until.you feel calm.

9. Meditate on the soles of your feet for about 10 to 15 min.

10. Slowly come out of your meditation, sit quietly for a few moments, and then resume your daily activities.

SOLE MEDITATION PRE AND POST RATING SCALE

SELF ASSESSMENT	RATING BEFORE MEDITATION (1-5)	RATING AFTER MEDITATION (1-5)
How Calm I Feel		
How Angry I Feel		
How Happy I Feel		
How Excited I Feel		
How Annoyed I Feel		
How Tired I Feel		
How _____ I Feel		

ALTERNATE NOSTRIL BREATHING TECHNIQUE

SANSKRIT NAME: *NADI SHODHANA*

*T*his breathing technique has been shown to calm the body by giving you control of your autonomic function…meaning it literally helps you calm yourself down and has been shown to be more effective for this purpose than other breathing techniques designed for the same purpose (e.g., paced breathing).

To practice ANB, fold your middle three fingers into your palm so only your thumb and pinky finger are extended. This is the universal sign for "call me," the Hawaiian sign for "hang loose," and my alma mater's sign for our mascot, the roadrunner.

Beep, beep.

Ahem, anyway. Use your thumb to close one nostril and breathe in through the other.

Move your hand to use your pinky to close the other nostril while releasing your thumb from the first nostril to breathe out.

Lather, rinse, repeat.

CHAIR YOGA

*T*hese are all bend-at-the-waist yoga forms that I specifically use to calm the vagus nerve and get the parasympathetic nervous system back online. They are all meant to be done seated. You can absolutely do these poses on a mat, but a chair can give you some good support, especially if don't have much yoga experience, have limited mobility, some pain issues, etc. But even in a chair, and even when not doing yoga forms that require extending the arms, you can still end up hurting yourself... and yoga is NOT supposed to hurt.

Some rules:

1) Don't do shit that hurts.

2) Modify whatever you need to modify so it doesn't hurt.

3) Don't do these exercises at 100% effort. Allow yourself the experience of only putting only 10% effort. Yoga works just as well (if not better) at 10% effort. Let yourself relax.

4) If you find yourself holding your breath, you're working too hard. You should be breathing because you are a human being and the breathing in and out thing is important, OK?

5) Use a chair that isn't on wheels, has a straight back, and (ideally) does not have arms).

6) Make sure you tell everyone that you totally did yoga today.

Mountain Pose

Sit straight up and extend your spine.

Root down in your chair on the lowest part of your tailbone (your sit bones)—the two points that take the weight of your body when you sit.

Be mindful to keep your legs at a 90 degree angle, with your knees directly over your ankles, with some space between your knees. This is a great pose to simply engage your core, check in with your posture, and focus on your breath. Come to this pose after each of the poses below.

Roll your shoulders back and pull your belly in toward your spine, then relax your arms down at your sides.

Cat-Cows

Keeping both feet on the floor and you spine long, put your hands on the tops of your thighs, or your knees if you can do so comfortably.

Arch your spine and roll your shoulders toward your back. Moo!

Round your spine, and drop your chin toward your chest, rolling your shoulders forward inward to your chest. Meow!

Continue moving back and forth between cat and cow positions, experimenting with moving during inhalations and exhalations, 5 to 10 cycles.

Sufi Rolls

As you inhale, lean your torso over to the right and then circle it out in front of you and around to the left, coming around the back as you exhale. Create a circle, leading from the belly button. Inhale forward and exhale backward. Then reverse.

Chair Pigeons

Move back into seated mountain, then bring your right ankle up to rest on your left thigh. Keep your knee parallel with your ankle as much as possible and hold this form for 5 breath cycles if you can do so without pain or discomfort. If you want to deepen the stretch, you can bend your waist forward over your leg. Repeat with the left leg.

Seated Forward Bend

Start back in seated mountain form, then fold your upper body over your legs from the waist. You can leave your hands at your sides or use them for extra support in the form by resting them on your thighs, then sliding them down your legs as you hinge forward. Experiment with holding this form for 5-10 cycles of breathing. When you are ready, move back into seated mountain form.

Single-Leg Stretch

For this one, you can scooch forward closer to the edge of the chair for more traction (but not so close you end up biffing it, ok?)

Stretch your right leg out, pointing your toes up and resting your heel on the floor. Rest your hands on your right leg, then lift up through your spine and bend over your right leg, sliding your hands down your leg to support your movement forward. You can take the stretch as far as it feels comfortable, but don't push yourself to the place of pain. You can hold onto your ankle or the back of your calf for support if you are able to drop that low. Hold this position for 5 breath cycles, if possible, and experiment with deepening the pose as you breathe.

Repeat with your left leg.

Final Relaxation Form

Sitting comfortably in your chair, drop all muscle tension. Close your eyes or allow your gaze to soft focus into the middle distance. Focus on your breath and notice sensations in your body. Allow yourself 2-3 minutes of rest before getting up from your practice.

Heal Yourself

SELF-EMPATHY

*E*mpathy asks us to recognize where someone is coming from. To "get it." It doesn't mean that every behavior is appropriate and permissible, it means we understand the cause and context. Put another way, it's the difference between nice and kind. Niceness lets us off the hook. Kindness understands how the hook came to be and supports our own process of getting unstuck from it.

Where self-compassion calls on us to give ourselves loving-kindness, self-empathy refers to our ability to understand our own perspective. There isn't a doing-anything with it, it's just letting yourself have a full emotional experience without self-recrimination and self-judgment.

It's one of those things that sounds really simple. But simple doesn't mean easy, especially when you are looking to separate out the part of yourself that has an experience from the metacognitive process of observing yourself have an experience.

In past books, I've written about self-empathy within the context of self-compassion, specifically using Marshall Rosenberg's conception of self-empathy as a framing for recognizing needs. But this is a little different and is based on the work of relational-cultural theorist Judy Jordan. It's a slightly more complex framing of self-empathy, asking us to suspend our presumptions about situations in order to allow ourselves to be complex and imperfect humans. From this place of openness, we then have the capacity to recognize how our anger (either internalized or externalized) is driving our responses so we can adjust as necessary.

To find a place of self-empathy, start by recognizing and naming the evaluations you are regularly making about yourself. Evaluations, after all, are judgements. And we are wired to make them. It's a feature not a bug of the human brain to look for cues of safety and unsafety, right? We evaluate situations constantly in order to protect ourselves. This practice helps us slow down our reaction process so we can "see" the evaluations before reacting to them. The evaluation may be a sense of irritation, a thought of "that's fucked up," or a tightness in one's chest, for example. It might also be an evaluation of our evaluation. Like finding ourselves irritated for being irritated, which then becomes a spiral of self-recrimination.

Self-evaluation

Now sit with the evaluation without trying to change it or alleviate it. Your only job is to observe your own process. Yes, that totally means I'm trying to trick you into a mindfulness practice. You caught me. You're looking to treat yourself with patience and to let yourself make evaluations

To quote the fantastic Sylvia Boorstein, *don't just do something, sit there.* You're paying attention to your patterns of evaluative judgements. You are a product of your experiences and you're doing a scientific study of how your personal experiences have impacted your own internal processes, allowing you to become proactive instead of reactive. This isn't to say you will never act on your evaluations. In fact, the next exercise, the six-step decision-making process, is a means of doing so more skillfully. Right now you're just looking at bringing more self-awareness to your own life.

Work with this process for a week. And make notes about the following:

What evaluations did you notice show up most regularly?

Are there any patterns to the situations you are experiencing and the evaluations you are making?

What about the evaluations of your evaluations? Did you notice that you beat yourself up for certain thoughts and feelings and somatic experiences that you were having?

What has been most effective in helping you slow down and provide yourself empathy to your own process?

Did you notice any shifts in how you decided to handle/tackle certain issues as you become more reflexive? How so?

SIX-STEP DECISION-MAKING PROCESS

Sometimes you're angry for a good reason. I mean :::gesticulates at the world around us::: I get it, and I feel the same way. Sometimes anger is telling us something really big needs to change. What's a solid way to figure out what change looks like? Being super cognizant of our decision-making processes.

Not all decisions are straightforward, right? If your choice is to be run over by a train or not run over by a train, chances are you will opt for the latter. But that isn't always the case. Deciding to stay with a partner in a tumultuous relationship or to stay in a job that is somewhat toxic but you really need the money, for example. Or how to be skillful in the face of a problem that needs resolution, whether interpersonal or societal.

This six-step decision-making process was detailed by legal consultant Nick Jarrett-Kerr, and I'm sharing it with y'all because I love his framing around our individual moral codes.

What is the biggest decision weighing on you right now?

1. Understand and center your own value system.

Our decisions should be rooted in what is important to us. We make better decisions in both the short and long term if we ground them in what is important to us and how we want to impact the world. If you value helping people over money at this point in your life, you won't do shady, harmful shit in the name of making a quick dollar, right?

What are your deeply-held values?

2. Identify all the realistic choices that are available to you.

Get clear on what all is possible and what is probable. Make a list of them. If you can narrow your choice pool to a handful of options, even better. Whenever possible, take time to sit with these choices and let yourself marinate on them a bit.

3. Take a deeper look at all of these choices.

Look at the best case scenarios, worst case scenarios, and the most likely outcomes of your choices.

What potential outcomes can you think of regarding your choices? How manageable is the worst thing that could happen? How can you mitigate risk?

4. Check in with your value system. Yes, again.

Back to our moral alignment. Do any of these options move us away from our value systems? Jarrett-Kerr articulates this check-in on alignment as a means of staying "anchored into a culture of conscious choices and decisions," demonstrating how constructs of moral codes show up in different world religions and how they can influence even our most secular and pragmatic pursuits, such as running a business. He points out that all our endeavors should remain tethered to what we believe about being a good human in the world, which he refers to as our "overall purpose." Our decision-making should reflect this throughout, right?

Which of the options you explored aligns best with who you want to be in the world?

5. Reflect on your motives and your current capacities.

Time for an ethics check-in here, once again. Make sure your motives are not focused solely on resolving discomfort/anxiety/stress caused by your personal circumstances or outside influences. If you only have 10 percent capacity right now, plan for that. Recognize that *is* your 100 percent. This helps you recognize issues that you may be avoiding because of your own overwhelm, and patterns of decision making that are influenced by your own load. This reflection isn't designed to have you "toughen up and work harder," but to work with clarity and vision so you can operate from your best self. Make notes about what you realize regarding motives and capacities in this situation.

6. Choose your choice, make your decision.

Your choice is your preference, noted. Your decision is your dedication to implementing this choice. These two are differentiated because it is important to be fully committed to your own plan, not letting the universe fling you around. Not making a choice is still a choice . . . and an active one. An active choice to give your power away. So why not remain empowered and be active on your own behalf? This is where you get practical about effecting change. And yes, of course, things won't work out perfectly. But I would always rather a failure exist as the result of being fully engaged and doing my level best than have it exist as a result of me not steering my own life.

What have you decided to do?

CHOOSING REST

So we all know that the amygdala is the feeling brain, meaning its job is to manage our emotional processing. The part you may-or-may-not know is that the amygdala plays an important role in managing our sleep. Researcher Yuki Motomura and team found that when sleep-deprived (*even by one night*) a physiological, functional deficit occurs between the amygdala and the ventral anterior cingulate cortex (vACC), which leads to a negative change in our mood (increases in depression, anxiety, and anger) and increases our responses to negative stimuli. Meaning, lack of sleep is directly causal to us being bigger assholes than we otherwise would be.

Of course, rest is more than just sleep, right? Dr. Saundra Dalton-Smith's book *Sacred Rest* (read it!) talks about all the ways we need more rest in our lives. This is your invitation to consider ways you can prioritize your own rest. And for extra credit? Track your mood after you are in the practice of rest and compare it to before. . . . see if you notice a difference.

Physical: Sleep and other restorative practices. Hot baths, gentle stretching, and restorative yoga are some of my physically restorative practices. Yours may be entirely different, so list them here.

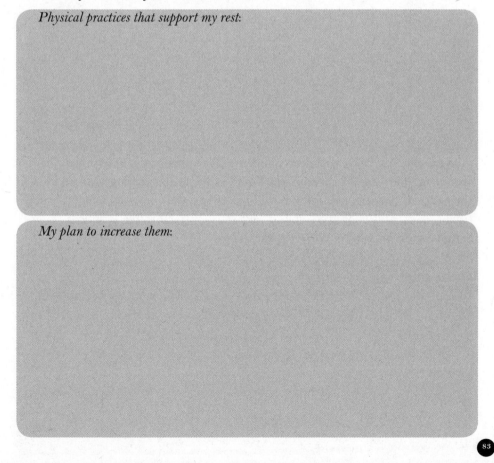

Physical practices that support my rest:

My plan to increase them:

Mental: Anything that slows down the computations your brain is up to in there. Reading a nice book with a guaranteed happy ending, playing solitaire, and feeding the ducks at the park are some of my mentally restorative practices. Yours may be entirely different, so list them here.

Mental practices that support my rest:

My plan to increase them:

Sensory: Anything that decreases the extra stimulation input in your environment. Turning off most of the lights in the room, driving with no music or podcasts playing, going for a walk before the sun comes up when it is still quiet, dark, and cool are some of my sensory restorative practices. Yours might be entirely different so list them here.

Sensory practices that support my rest:

My plan to increase them:

Creative: Anything that helps you slow down enough to appreciate the beauty of the natural world and the beauty we create. Watching the sun come up, going hiking, going to museums, flipping through art books, and listening to music are some of my creative restorative practices. Yours might be entirely different so list them here:

Creative practices that support my rest:

My plan to increase them:

Emotional: Anything that gives you space to slow down and feel your emotions. Journaling, dancing, mindfulness meditation, and talking to a loving friend who gets it but will still gently call me on my bullshit are some of my emotional restorative practices. Yours might be entirely different so list them here.

Emotional practices that support my rest:

My plan to increase them:

Social: Anything that gives you needed rest or alone time *and* time with the people who nourish you. I plan my weeks around ensuring some alone time, which may be reading in bed with a cat or wandering a thrift store by myself. I also love planning non-pressure-filled activities with peovple I enjoy being around. Upcoming from when I am writing this, I'm throwing a "no-bra dinner" where everyone gets to come over dressed comfy, and we will eat tons of snacks (we can call it charcuterie if we want to be bougie) and hang out.

Your social restorative practices may be entirely different so list them here.

Social practices that support my rest:

My plan to increase them:

Spiritual: I love the definition of spirituality as "purposeful belonging." For me, smudging, meditating, and speaking with the elders are all spiritual practices, and so is finding ways to care for others and the world. Your spiritual restorative practices may be entirely different, so list them here.

Spiritual practices that support my rest:

My plan to increase them:

MOOD TRACKER

WEEKLY MOOD TRACKER

AM I IN A BAD MOOD OR...
DO YOU SUCK?

	MOOD	SITUATION	MAGNITUDE (0-100)	SYMPTOMS
SUNDAY				
MONDAY				
TUESDAY				
WEDNESDAY				
THURSDAY				
FRIDAY				
SATURDAY				

WEEKLY MOOD TRACKER

AM I IN A BAD
MOOD OR…
DO YOU SUCK?

	MOOD	SITUATION	MAGNITUDE (0–100)	SYMPTOMS
SUNDAY				
MONDAY				
TUESDAY				
WEDNESDAY				
THURSDAY				
FRIDAY				
SATURDAY				

WEEKLY MOOD TRACKER

AM I IN A BAD MOOD OR... DO YOU SUCK?

	MOOD	SITUATION	MAGNITUDE (0-100)	SYMPTOMS
SUNDAY				
MONDAY				
TUESDAY				
WEDNESDAY				
THURSDAY				
FRIDAY				
SATURDAY				

THE CYCLE OF EMOTIONAL REGULATION

We've talked a lot about how we become dysregulated, so it's time to talk about how we can remain regulated. It's hard work and takes a ton of practice. Consider that we are aiming for equanimity, not perfection. It's not always possible, but well worth the effort for ourselves and those around us.

The cycle has four parts.

Notice and Name: This just means recognizing that you are experiencing an emotion and defining what it is to you. This may be harder to parse out at first. "Dude, I'm just mad!" is an entirely good answer. With time, you may detect more subtleties, such as "I'm frustrated" or "I'm discontent" instead. The minute we can become metacognitive (aware of our own cognitive processes) the better we become at managing them.

Accept: This is as hard, if not harder, than step one. We tend to self-shame around uncomfortable emotions. We aren't "supposed" to feel angry, right? Or was that just my parents? Accepting your feelings doesn't mean they are accurate, and doesn't mean you have to be reactive because of them. It just means acknowledging their existence. Emotions are information from your body designed to protect you . . . they're just trying to do their jobs.

Get curious: Once you accept the emotion, listen to what it is trying to tell you. What thoughts and urges are you experiencing? What's going on in your body? What else is your brain telling you right now?

Allow and Release: Allowing means letting the emotion exist and release refers to letting go of the urge to fight its existence. This is a form of "Yes, I'm furious . . . and I'm not gonna act a fool about it," not an "I release my fury and embrace calm," or whatever. The emotion itself will release in its own time and its own way because you listened and tended to your internal signals.

Next time you're feeling something big, take a moment, either in the thick of it or immediately after, and go through the cycle with the help of this flow chart:

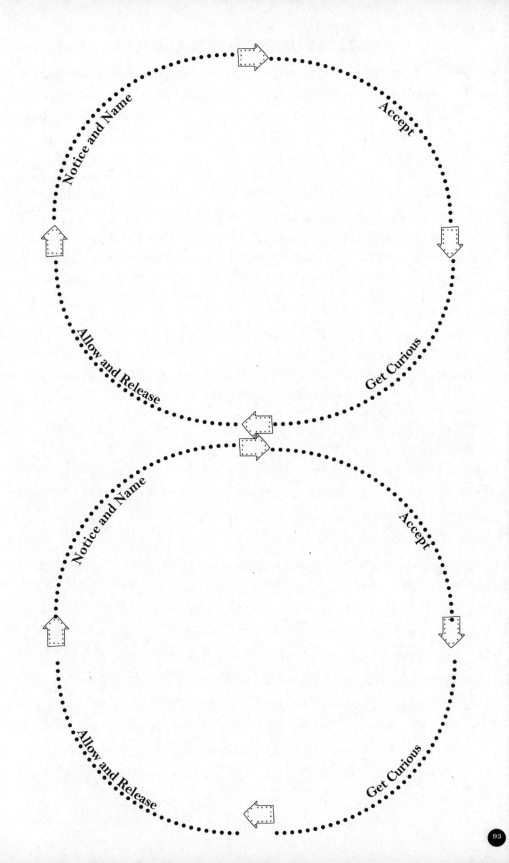

GRATITUDE JOURNALING

Gratitude helps us build more positive relationships, reduces depression, increases resilience, improves our physical health, increases empathy, decreases depression, and improves quality and quantity of sleep, to name just a few research findings. What do these things have to do with anger management? Everything, right? These are all foundational markers of well-being that help us be our best (not mean, angry, reactive) selves. There is a huge amount of research around gratitude and how helpful it is for our mental well-being.

How so? Gratitude journaling activates two different parts of the brain, the hypothalamus (stress regulator) and the ventral tegmental area (the reward system activator). So at the same time we are reducing stress, we are creating the sensation of winning a (little, tiny) lottery by increasing serotonin and dopamine—which is why some gratitude researchers call gratitude a "natural antidepressant."

Gratitude journaling seems to work best when you don't do it exactly the same way every day—it's good to build a habit, but if it becomes too much of a habit, the benefits decrease over time. So we've provided a bunch of prompts below. You can fill out a different one every day or a couple times a week, or copy them into a journal you are going to use in the longer term.

Small, daily comforts I am grateful for

Material items that make my life easier that I am grateful for

Beauty in the world that I am grateful for

Kindness of others that I am grateful for

My healthy stress management skills that I am grateful for

New skills I have learned that I am grateful for

Tasks I have accomplished that I am grateful for

Future plans I have created that I am grateful for

Ways I have demonstrated compassion that I am grateful for

Self-care strategies I have used that I am grateful for

Positive thinking changes that I am grateful for

Healthy boundaries I have developed that I am grateful for

RELATIONAL IMAGES ABOUT ANGER

*A*nger is something that comes on quickly (because in truly dangerous situations, we don't and shouldn't have time to think about it), so we often miss some of the underlying patterns in our processes. And generally these patterns were created and reinforced in relationships. Meaning we believe something about ourselves because other people believe them about us. Or we think they do. Or expect them to, based on past relationships.

Aaron Beck, the founder of Cognitive Behavioral Therapy, used the term "core beliefs" to describe the ideas we perceive to be fundamentally true about ourselves. His focus was on the profound core beliefs, such as "I am worthless," that feed emotional health issues and how these beliefs are built through our thoughts and the rules we create about the world.

Within Relational-Cultural Therapy (RCT), however, the thinking is slightly different. RCT theorists focus on our deep need for connection that often becomes at odds with our need for self-protection based on our past hurts, violations, and disappointments.

Because RCT focuses on humans as existing in relationship with others, they propose that instead of formulating core beliefs, we form "relational images." Our relational images are based on our past experiences of what happens when we reach out for connection, including our expectations and fears as well as our hopes. It is how we can narrate a whole exchange with another person solely within our own heads, without their actual participation.

This exercise is incredibly helpful in catching our own relational image patterns. I'm starting with some directly related to anger and its siblings, but you can also use it for other emotional content.

If I express frustration, other people will

If I feel angry, other people will

If I'm aggressive, other people will

If I do/think/feel/say _____ *, other people will*

If I do/think/feel/say _____ *, other people will*

If I do/think/feel/say _____ , *other people will*

If I do/think/feel/say _____ , *other people will*

If I do/think/feel/say _____ , *other people will*

If I do/think/feel/say _____ , *other people will*

If I do/think/feel/say _____ , *other people will*

COMMUNICATING WITH "I STATEMENTS"

Now here is a great fucking tool for communicating your action plan to resolve your feelings with someone else. You may decide to share these statements with someone. Or you may just be doing internal work around your own anger patterns. Acknowledgement isn't necessarily done in your out-loud voice.

I feel _____

when you _____

What I want is _____

I feel _____

when you _____

What I want is _____

I feel _____

when you _____

What I want is _____

I feel _____

when you _____

What I want is _____

I feel _____

when you _____

What I want is _____

I feel _____

when you _____

What I want is _____

FORGIVENESS

Maybe there's some person (or some group of people) you're angry at, and maybe they totally deserve it. And maybe they don't even want to be forgiven because they don't think they did a damn thing wrong (this group of people is often referred to as a legislative body). But how pissed are you? Is it fucking you up? You deserve some relief, even if they don't deserve forgiveness.

Forgiveness isn't about forgetting what people did and/or letting them be shitty to you in the future. That's not forgiveness . . . that's "how to be a doormat," and we are no such thing. This is just the internal process it takes to decouple yourself from what happened so you aren't continuing to exhaust yourself with anger.

Just like with any other emotional work, there is no finite endpoint in forgiveness. We may end up back in the process at any time, having to work through things yet again. And that's okay. It's a fundamental part of the human experience and of having an overprotective brain that is always remembering the past as an indicator of our possible future.

So I looked at the research on the process of forgiveness and created a stage-wise model to help conceptualize how it works. Because knowing where we are and what we are working is incredibly helpful. It normalizes the process when we are feeling frustrated, stuck, and broken. And it gives us a framework for moving forward from those same feelings of frustration, stuckness, and brokenness. It's a reminder that all hard work is a process and that the process is never truly complete.

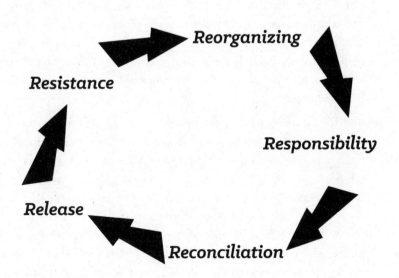

Resistance: This is probably the most self-explanatory part of the model. It's about our own resistance to forgiving someone who has harmed us. If we are holding onto a strong, negative emotion like anger, there is a really good reason we have it. It means we were hurt by something quite badly, and there is generally a person or people that hurt us—some fucker caused our suffering. The idea of letting go of that anger feels counterintuitive to protecting ourselves from more hurt in the future.

Reorganizing: In this stage, we start to really process all the parts of the situation. We have to unpack all our shit around it. What was done to us, the hows and whys of the circumstances, which aspects of the situation belong to others and which belong to us. Every situation has context and this stage is when we start realizing that there is far more to the situation than the story we have been telling ourselves about the person or people who hurt us. This may mean reconsidering intent or other outside influences. For example, knowing someone's abuse history doesn't excuse how they hurt you, but it can really change the context around why they treated you the way they did.

Responsibility: OK, this is the hard shit. This is a conversation between your rational, higher self and your wounded, protected emotional self. And that conversation involves taking responsibility for your own emotional content. Others are accountable for their behavior, but the only person accountable for my response is me. That hardly seems fair when people are being truly awful but there is also an extreme freedom in realizing that the one power that no one can take from me in any situation is the power of my own response. Taking responsibility for my own response means taking ownership of my life back. It means untethering myself from a chain of shitty, coercive, or abusive behavior by someone else. There is a real badassery in that.

Reconciliation: Reconciliation is the act of making one thing compatible with another. We have to reconcile our emotional content with the harmful behaviors we engage in because of it. Even if we aren't taking it out on anyone else, the continued rumination and angry thoughts are hurting us, right? And we have to reconcile our actions with our internal moral center . . . with who we know ourselves to be. I haven't met anyone who considers themselves a pissed off, vengeful person. Everyone I have ever talked to considers themselves a peaceful person who just wants to be happy. So we have to reconcile our anger and how we react from it with that internal peaceful person.

Release: If the other parts seemed hard, this is the absolute worst. This is the part of the process where our realization of the mismatch between our internal self and our continued emotional state requires action. We are hurting ourselves and others. This doesn't mean giving up on working for change if change needs to happen. It definitely doesn't mean you need to let people who hurt you stomp all over you again. It means that the protective burst of anger that propelled you to safety is no longer necessary. And continuing to hold on to the anger and developing a long-term angry mood serves only a continued source of pain for us. Only with releasing that anger, can we truly move on and reconnect with our inner, peaceful nature.

So how do we, you know, actually do the thing? Forgive someone?

Because forgiveness is such a complicated process (especially when the person we are forgiving doesn't give a fuck, and we're doing it solely for our own benefit) it is usually easier to start by reverse engineering a time in our past where we have been through this process already, so we can look at how we did it. It's like brain hacking our future processes by looking at how we were successful in the past.

Start by briefly describing the incident and the person you worked to forgive.

For each stage, list what helped get you through that portion of the process. What did you learn? What can you carry forward as a tool later?

Resistance

Reorganizing

Responsibility

Reconciliation

Release

AUTHENTIC APOLOGY

Forgiveness is a universal human need. It is a topic for consideration in all religious texts and many philosophical ones (Immanuel Kant most notably). It's one of the eight positive emotions, according to psychiatrist George Vaillant. (And guess what? Compassion is another of the eight).

Forgiveness often sets the stage for relationship repair. The last exercise was about forgiving others; here we are focusing on requesting forgiveness.

A true apology is as rare as unpolluted urban air. The three most popular apology formats are also deeply shitty:

- The dismiss and move forward ("Stop being upset; you're too sensitive; it was funny!")

- The political no-responsibility apology ("I'm sorry if people were upset.")

- The half-assed sorry/not sorry apology. ("I'm sorry I upset you; it was just a joke!")

Apologizing is difficult because true accountability requires a level of vulnerability with which we are deeply uncomfortable. Anyone doing the difficult work of authentic apologizing has my deepest respect.

My model of an authentic apology is a three Rs model: **Responsibility**, **Recognition**, and **Repair**.

Responsibility refers to ownership of the harm caused without explanation or equivocation. No "buts," no "I didn't mean it" (I'm gonna presume you didn't mean it, at least the vast majority of the time). Just "I see that my words/actions (or lack thereof) caused pain. Because they were my words/actions (or lack thereof), I am responsible for that pain, and I am sorry that I caused it."

Recognition is where we open ourselves to a deeper understanding of the harm we caused. Of course, we cannot force someone to hear or accept an apology from us, and we definitely cannot force them to revisit the issue in detail, but we can invite them into a dialogue in which we learn more and grow more as humans. We might ask, "If you are willing to share more about how my words/actions (or lack thereof) hurt you, I would like to hear you. I am committed to working on myself as a human being, which means more listening and understanding." If the person is willing to tell us, we shut up and commit to listening without intending to respond. Recognition gives us the context surrounding our harm, allowing us to better generalize the lesson to other aspects of our lives.

Repair is where the real relationship work happens, according to Relational-Cultural Theory. Disconnection and conflict are an unavoidable part of relationships, and they can lead to further alienation or they can be our opportunity to do the vulnerable work of repair. Where a facetious or dismissive apology creates anger and shame, repair creates authenticity, empathy, and growth. Repair isn't only atonement. Acknowledging that you hear and confirm how your actions have affected someone else is repair. Showing someone that you believe their experience is real can help make them whole again. Repair is where you say, "Now I see the specific ways that what I did/said (or didn't) hurt you. I am so sorry, and here is a specific example of something I will do differently in the future." And then, you do the different thing.

Now write your own apology utilizing the three Rs. It's better to keep it short, lest you ramble into dangerous territory or make excuses. So give it some good thought and re-read the above before you start writing.

What is the situation you need to craft an apology for?

How will you accept responsibility?

How will you make space for recognition?

If the person accepts your offer to listen and learn, how will you repair?

If you did complete the apology process, what happened next? Did you learn something that surprised you? What will you change in the future?

If you weren't able to complete the apology process, why not? Did you learn anything to take into future apologies?

ATONEMENT AND ACCOUNTABILITY

While authentic apologies are powerful work, you also may be recognizing some larger patterns across relationships in your life. And you may decide that casting your repair process out more widely is also important to your healing, those you love, and the world in general. This also may provide a solid starting point when the person to whom you want to apologize isn't amenable to a personal conversation with you.

In order to look at this work holistically, let's borrow from a four-thousand-year-old tradition. Scholars of Judaism note significant differences between the terms "atonement," "forgiveness," and "repentance," which are incredibly helpful to our discussion here, if only as a philosophical stance. Meaning, you don't have to celebrate Passover or worship any deities to find this helpful to your own internal work.

Repentance in Hebrew is "tshuva" which means *return*. So when we discuss our value system and moral alignment, think of repentance as *a return to alignment*. It minimizes our risk of causing more harm in the future and is, therefore, considered *the work of ethical self-transformation*. We can always grow and change and become better even though we can't often undo past harm. We can take responsibility, repair as much as possible, and do better in the future.

Forgiveness is the hoped-for outcome of our expression of regret through apologies like the one in the last exercise. Forgiveness isn't something we can force from others, but we can create a space that may be conducive to them doing so.

Atonement consists of the actions we take beyond our apology to create healing. Repentance is our internal repair work; atonement is the external expression of that work.

Repentance work is a lengthy process, not just a tearful voicemail (or press conference, as the case may be).

Rabbi Danya Ruttenberg explains the steps to repentance work as follows. For each one, explain how you could achieve it and how it fits your specific situation.

1. *Owning the harm perpetrated (ideally, publicly to your community, and in a way that protects the privacy of affected individuals who want that).*

2. Doing the work to become the kind of person who doesn't do harm (which requires a ton of inner work).

3. Making restitution for harm done, in whatever way possible.

4. Then apologizing for the harm caused in whatever way that will make it as right as possible with the victim.

5. Making a better choice when faced with the opportunity to cause similar harm in the future.

~Diagnosing Anger~

ANGER AND MENTAL HEALTH DIAGNOSES

*W*hile anger responses are associated with many mental health issues (as well as just, you know, being alive) there are five in particular in which anger is a key component of the diagnostic criteria, according to a 2016 journal article by psychology researchers Ephrem Fernandez and Sheri L. Johnson. If the expressions of anger you are concerned about seem particularly difficult to manage, seeing if any of these diagnoses fit your experience may be an incredibly helpful starting point for treatment options.

These diagnoses are drawn from the fifth edition of the Diagnostic and Statistical Manual of Mental Disorders (DSM-5-TR), which is the official list of diagnosable mental health issues that clinicians use. I've included specific diagnostic codes not just for the clinicians reading this but for anyone working to decipher their own medical records.

There is space for you to make your own notes as well as jot down any questions you want to bring to a treatment provider should you be seeking a diagnosis and/or care.

Intermittent Explosive Disorder (312.34 [F63.81])

This is the DSM-5 diagnosis most directly related to someone's anger. It is operationalized as someone who is regularly angry and impulsively aggressive out of proportion to circumstances. This part is important, because Intermittent Explosive Disorder (IED) is considered an impulse control disorder.

- Earlier versions of the DSM noted that individuals with IED were generally mild mannered but then went ka-boom on the regular. This is no longer part of the diagnostic criteria. Now, someone *could* be pretty chill until they pop off, but they are equally likely to be a lower-level crank until they pop off, with the important part remaining that the anger responses aren't *chronic*.

- The DSM-5 also expanded diagnostic criteria to include non-physical aggression, like tirades and tantrums.

• Diagnosis is based on frequency and severity, though other researchers have called to also consider duration of anger responses, latency of responses, and threshold to responses as important means to differentiate IED from other presentations of anger.

• IED has been correlated with an early childhood history of parental under-involvement (read: milder neglect), lack of care, childhood trauma, and childhood physical abuse (but not sexual or emotional abuse, likely because these types of abuse are more strongly correlated with internalizing symptoms than externalizing symptoms).

• The individual being diagnosed must be at least six years old (chronologically or developmentally) to receive this diagnosis.

• We also get pretty granular on how common and severe the outbursts are. If it is verbal aggression or non-damaging or injurious physical aggression, the DSM states they must happen at least twice weekly (on average) over a period of at least three months. If the physical aggression is causing injury or damage, it has to have occurred three times within a twelve-month period.

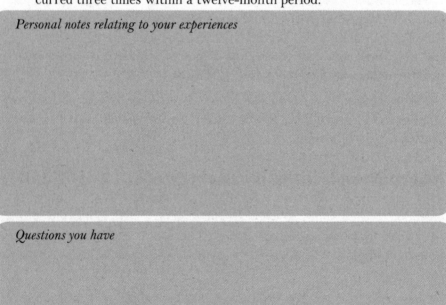

Personal notes relating to your experiences

Questions you have

Oppositional Defiant Disorder (313.81 [F91.3])

Oppositional Defiant Disorder (ODD) is defined as "a pattern of angry/irritable mood, argumentative/defiant behavior, or vindictiveness" as evidenced by at least four of eight symptoms listed. Two of the symptom criteria specifically reference anger (being angry, losing temper) and the others are suggestive of anger (being annoyed, being argumentative, etc.). The major difference between ODD and IED is that individuals with ODD are not as aggressive in their behaviors.

- There is no minimum age listed as part of the diagnostic criteria, but the DSM does note that if the individual is under five years old, the symptoms must be present almost daily. And if they are over five years old, almost weekly. It is rare that ODD is diagnosed in teens and adults, but you may see it in treatment records if it was diagnosed in a younger kiddo who is still struggling with symptoms. The idea being, we are looking for it being present often enough that it is a disorder of temperament, not a regular fluctuation of mood.

- Research suggests that many people with ODD lack insight into their own role. Meaning they see their responses as normal and justified to circumstances.

- ODD does not require symptoms showing across life domains. Meaning, if it only happens at home or at school or at work, it can still be diagnosed. But let me put on my clinical trainer hat for the other diagnosticians out there. If *any* behavior is only happening in one life domain, please explore what the hell is going on in that life domain before assigning a diagnosis. A shitty, verbally abusive teacher causing enormous problems for someone in their classroom should be dealt with, rather than shoving a label on a frustrated, overwhelmed kiddo.

- It is also important that the behaviors aren't related to tasks that require sustained effort and attention. If that is when the outbursts occur, you are far more likely looking at neurodiversity overwhelm, not a temperament disorder.

- ODD has been tied to a maladaptive caregiver cycle. Authority figures and caregivers responding to a child's non-compliance may exacerbate their non-compliance, creating a continuous cycle of activation. So this isn't to say parents or other caregivers "started it," but adults who struggle to handle temperament issues skillfully can unintentionally elevate a problematic situation.

- Researchers have also demonstrated, however, that ODD also has some relation to serotonin transporter genetic polymorphism; therefore, it likely has a genetic component.

Personal notes relating to your experiences

Questions you have

Disruptive Mood Dysregulation Disorder (296.99[F34.8])

Disruptive mood dysregulation disorder (DMDD) is used to diagnose temper outbursts that occur three or more times a week, with irritability and anger being presented most days and this situation has been ongoing for more than a year. DMDD was introduced in the DSM-5 as a depressive disorder, so we have significantly less research than we do on the other diagnoses associated with anger.

- The diagnosis should not be made on anyone under the age of six, or over the age of eighteen. And the symptoms should have been present before age ten, even if the diagnosis is made later.

- Much of the criteria associated with DMDD is based on the work of Leibenluft and colleagues, who had been studying what they termed severe mood dysregulation (SMD) in children that didn't meet criteria for bipolar disorder and didn't have a genetic predisposition to bipolar disorder, so there was likely something else going on. Their laboratory studies found that children with this diagnosis show greater psychophysiological response to tasks designed to be frustrating and had different neurological responses to viewing faces that displayed anger. Which is all to say there is a level of sensitivity that is likely more innate than inculcated.

• That being said, there is a good amount of overlap between DMDD, ADHD, and ODD, so how this diagnosis plays out may change with more time and research.

Personal notes relating to your experiences

Questions you have

Borderline Personality Disorder (301.83 (F60. 3])

Borderline personality disorder (BPD) is a diagnosis that is most recognized for how much it disrupts our ability to regulate our own emotions. The DSM-5 marked a big change in how diagnoses are categorized. Personality disorders used to be categorized differently than diagnoses that were considered biochemically induced (like bipolar disorder). Diagnoses like BPD were considered behavioral. Which is a rude-ass way of saying you're "acting crazy," but it isn't based on neurological differences. Further research shows that that's whole, entire bullshit, and it's just as biochemical as anything else. In fact, some research is now suggesting that BPD is a form of neurodiversity, which entirely makes sense to me, and it's changed how I approach treatment. But all that aside, let's talk about how it is diagnosed.

- You can be diagnosed with BPD without having any anger criteria met, though it is rare. In order to meet diagnostic criteria, you have to meet at least five of the nine markers of BPD listed in the DSM. One is specific to anger outbursts ("inappropriate intense anger") and one is commonly related to anger (affective instability, sometimes manifested as irritability). BPD is considered an anger-related diagnosis because these two markers are considered the most common and hardest to manage manifestations of BPD.

- While you can qualify for a BPD diagnosis without these two markers, both are strongly correlated with the other diagnostic criteria, specifically the ones regarding suicidality and "self-destructive" behavior.

- Research around certain aspects of anger found that the intensity of anger isn't higher among individuals with BPD, but the temporal aspect (meaning how long it lasts) is. I see this as another indicator that it is a form of neurodiversity.

- The diagnostic criteria also emphasize that the anger is often triggered specifically by interpersonal conflict (unlike with IED) and is tethered most often to feelings of rejection and abandonment (real or perceived).

- Other research shows that individuals with BPD misread cues from others regularly, specifically thinking others are angry at them when they are not.

Personal notes relating to your experiences

Bipolar Disorder (multiple codes available, depending on type)

When we think of bipolar disorder as quick movements between deep depressions and huge bouts of energy and happiness, the reality is that the periods of elevated mood can also be exhibited through excessive anger. Several factor analysis studies have shown that anger is a core facet of manic symptoms, far more so than "ran off to Vegas to marry this person I just met last night at Denny's."

- The anger associated with BD is especially evident in children and teens during manic episodes.

- It's present during depressive episodes as well. People with BD experience twice the anger in these states as people with unipolar depression.

- Other research demonstrates that regardless of episode status, anger is far more common among individuals with BD than the rest of the population, even when otherwise stable. In these states, the individual may not be behaviorally reactive, but they are aware that their internal experience of anger is outsized to the situation.

Personal notes relating to your experiences

Questions you have

Questions for Consideration

Was there any diagnosis that you feel may fit your current situation?

Is there any diagnosis you've seen assigned to you or a loved one that you think may not be accurate?

What specifically do you want to review with a clinician?

SELF-INJURY CHECKLIST

Research shows, time and again, that individuals with elevated levels of internalized anger—anger at the people who have hurt us and anger at ourselves for being helpless in the face of abuse—are the people who engage in self-injurious behavior.

I've found in my practice that not everyone understands their behaviors as intentional self-injury, so I've included a checklist. If you have a suspicion that some of your behaviors toward your own body are self-injurious, or if you are realizing that your self-harm behavior is connected to trauma and internalized rage, therapy can really help your healing.

(This worksheet was adapted From The Cornell Research Program on Self-Injurious Behaviors in Adolescents and Young Adults)

○ Scratched or tore at your skin enough that you tore the skin or left a mark that lasted more than a few minutes

○ Pinched your skin enough that you left a mark that lasted more than a few minutes

○ Cut or carved any of the flesh on your body with any form of sharp object (razor blade, knife, scissors, sharp glass, broken button, broken CD, etc.)

○ Ripped or torn any of the flesh on your body

○ Burned any of the flesh on your body

○ Intentionally exposed your flesh to caustic or acidic substances

○ Ingested poisonous, toxic, or otherwise harmful substances or items

○ Injected poisonous or toxic substances into your flesh or blood steam for their harmful effect (not for a high, like with drugs)

○ Broken or attempted to break your own bones

○ Stuck pins or needles anywhere in or underneath your skin (other than piercings, tattoos, or BDSM needle play)

○ Punched yourself, punched objects, or banged other parts of your body into objects to the point of causing injury (bruising, swelling, bleeding, inflammation, marks that last more than a few minutes)

○ Intentionally kept wounds from healing by picking at them, irritating them, digging at them, rubbing toxic substances on them, etc.

○ Engaged in fighting, roughhousing, sports, or other aggressive activities for the intention of hurting yourself (e.g., taking hits or falls you didn't need to take)

○ Jumped down from an unsafe distance for the intention of taking a hard fall

○ Ripped or pulled out hair from your flesh

○ Starved yourself or undernourished yourself not in an attempt to control weight or body shape, but as self punishment.

○ Torn out your fingernails or toenails

○ Choked yourself for the injury or to pass out (not for the high or for autoerotic asphyxiation)

Are there any other ways you have purposely physically hurt yourself or intentionally mutilated your body in order to hurt yourself?

PERSONAL SYMPTOM RECORD

Anger, anxiety, and mood disorders don't show up on lab tests. To get help for them, you'll usually need to get your own damn self into a clinic saying "shit is fucked and I really really need to figure this out and get help" so that someone can help you sort through the shit and figure out what was wrong. And that's what this worksheet is for. Not for you to self-diagnose then demand Xanax from your doc, but for you to take time to create a good record of what's been going on so you can connect with a clinician who can ask good questions, clarify information, and help you figure out what treatment and support you need…and hopefully in far less than ten fucking years. So consider using this and bringing it in to your appointment and requesting to go through it with your treatment provider.

What does "symptoms" mean? Anything that you are thinking, feeling, and doing that are reinforcing problems or stuckness in your life instead of growth and healing.

(Exercise on next page)

Symptoms I'm having	Intensity of the experience (on a scale of 1-10)	How long, on average, do I experience the symptom when I have it?	How often do I experience the symptom in any given week?	How many months or years has this been going on?

ABUSE RED FLAGS

Anger is an emotion, and aggression is the action that it motivates in many people. When aggression (physical or otherwise) is consistently directed at another person, it may be abuse.

Abuse, according to the Oxford English Dictionary, is when we treat people with cruelty and/or violence, especially when it is a regular and repeated occurrence. Abusive behavior is most marked by the coercive control, not the physical actions (which I wrote about extensively in my book *Unfuck Your Boundaries*). And these behaviors don't show up in full force when you're still in a new relationship. Which means we need to be better at looking for red flags as possible warnings that someone has potential for abuse, based on these early behaviors that steer into coercive control.

Obviously, many of these behaviors can be due to other reasons, like mental health issues that need treatment, neurodiversity, misunderstanding cues and roles, substance issues, and plain old just being excited to be with you and being kind of a pain about it. But even the most benign of reasons needs to be addressed, not allowed. Can they take accountability and make changes to be a healthier partner? Can they respect boundaries? Their responses can help signal if this is an ongoing and possibly escalating problem.

If you think you might be in an abusive relationship with a partner, date, family member, friend, boss, or someone else, you can start the process of getting help by calling the National Domestic Violence Hotline at 1-800-799-7233 (SAFE), 1-800-787-3224 (TTY), or texting START to 88788 (SMS).

If you are concerned that your own behaviors are abusive towards another person or people, you can start getting help through the same numbers. And you are amazing for taking responsibility for yourself and starting the journey to healing.

This abuse red flags list is based on work produced by the WomenStrength Program, the Safehouse Progressive Alliance for Nonviolence, and the Verizon HopeLine.

For each entry, indicate if someone in your past behaved this way towards you, someone is currently treating you in this way, if you have treated someone this way in the past, or if you are treating someone this way now.

◯ *Someone Else - Past* | ◯ *Someone Else - Current* | ◯ *Me - Past* | ◯ *Me - Current*

Jealousy and Possessiveness: This can include not wanting you around people they consider a sexual threat and accusing you of cheating on them. It can also include wanting to be with you constantly (and getting upset if you are spending time with others instead of them), checking in on you constantly, asking others to check in on you, and wanting to track you all the time "for safety" (and I don't mean because you are going hiking and might get stuck).

○ *Someone Else - Past* | ○ *Someone Else - Current* | ○ *Me - Past* | ○ *Me - Current*
Gaslighting: This is a hot-button of a term nowadays, and it gets misrepresented regularly. Gaslighting is an intentional psychological manipulation sustained over time, designed to question your own experiences. This isn't the partner having a different memory of a conversation and disagreeing with you, it is a partner who can be shown the receipts and still deny reality.

○ *Someone Else - Past* | ○ *Someone Else - Current* | ○ *Me - Past* | ○ *Me - Current*
Controlling Behavior: Similar to the above, but maybe less in the immediate moment. Questioning what you do, who you are with, where you went, what you wore, what you ate, what you talked about. They want you to ask for permission to do certain things or work to convince you you don't make good decisions. Like above, it may be couched in being concerned for your safety when your safety isn't a real concern.

○ *Someone Else - Past* | ○ *Someone Else - Current* | ○ *Me - Past* | ○ *Me - Current*
Quick Involvement: Love-bombing level of early commitment. Wanting to live together, get engaged, get married within a few months and pressuring you to make that commitment even if you have some hesitation.

○ *Someone Else - Past* | ○ *Someone Else - Current* | ○ *Me - Past* | ○ *Me - Current*
Unrealistic Expectations: They expect perfection or treat you like you are perfect, doing so in a way that sets you up to perform to their standards or fail as a partner if/when you are unable to do so. Some isolation tactics fall under this umbrella, such as "I don't need friends, I have you" and maybe following up with, "You don't need anyone else, you have me.

○ *Someone Else - Past* | ○ *Someone Else - Current* | ○ *Me - Past* | ○ *Me - Current*
Isolation: Other isolation tactics may include putting down all the people you know, making judgements about them, and telling you that you don't need these people in your life. They say that other people are too controlling, aren't operating at your level, just trying to use you or have sex with you, or are always trying to get you in trouble. They may even impede you going to school and/or work. With time, you lose the resources of having others in your life as they continue to pull you away from others.

○ *Someone Else - Past* | ○ *Someone Else - Current* | ○ *Me - Past* | ○ *Me - Current*
Blames Others for Their Own Problematic Behaviors and Their Consequences: They don't demonstrate accountability for their problems at work, school, in any of their relationships (including with you).

○ *Someone Else - Past* | ○ *Someone Else - Current* | ○ *Me - Past* | ○ *Me - Current*

Blames Others for Their Own Feelings and Their Consequences: They don't demonstrate accountability for their feelings. They tell you that your behavior makes them hurt or makes them angry, therefore you should change it. This pairs well with the lack of accountability for the problems their behaviors create.

○ *Someone Else - Past* | ○ *Someone Else - Current* | ○ *Me - Past* | ○ *Me - Current*

Hypersensitivity: They view all feedback as a personal attack, are easily insulted, blow things out of proportion, blow up regularly, and are often unpredictable.

○ *Someone Else - Past* | ○ *Someone Else - Current* | ○ *Me - Past* | ○ *Me - Current*

Disrespectful or Cruel: They are insensitive and disrespectful to others, especially those with less power than them. Like being rude to workers, punishing children, or being cruel to animals. They are insensitive to the experiences of others and dismiss their own actions in these regards as justified.

○ *Someone Else - Past* | ○ *Someone Else - Current* | ○ *Me - Past* | ○ *Me - Current*

Forceful During Sexual Activity: They are pushy and aggressive about sexual intimacy, sulk and pout when you don't comply, or use anger to scare you into compliance. They may also make comments/jokes about your body, your sexuality, or your value as a partner in order to encourage you to "perform" for them.

○ *Someone Else - Past* | ○ *Someone Else - Current* | ○ *Me - Past* | ○ *Me - Current*

Rigid Gender Roles: They believe dismissive things about your gender, specifically that it is inferior. Or that you should perform certain roles in certain ways.

○ *Someone Else - Past* | ○ *Someone Else - Current* | ○ *Me - Past* | ○ *Me - Current*

Sudden Mood Swings: They swing from sweet and nice to incredibly angry or incredibly sad with no warning or context.

○ *Someone Else - Past* | ○ *Someone Else - Current* | ○ *Me - Past* | ○ *Me - Current*

Doesn't Respect Your Property or Privacy: They go through your stuff, including your phone/computer/etc. Things that they don't like (pictures of other people, clothes they don't approve of, etc., may start disappearing).

○ *Someone Else - Past* | ○ *Someone Else - Current* | ○ *Me - Past* | ○ *Me - Current*

Self-Centered: They focus on their wants and needs over your own. You may acquiesce to eating where and what they want, watching what they want, wearing what they want, etc.

○ *Someone Else - Past* | ○ *Someone Else - Current* | ○ *Me - Past* | ○ *Me - Current*

Double Standards: This could be any behavior that is allowable for them but not for you. Staying out late with friends, spending money, etc. It could also be about degrading your past behaviors while theirs were similar (partying, number of sexual partners, etc.).

○ *Someone Else - Past* | ○ *Someone Else - Current* | ○ *Me - Past* | ○ *Me - Current*

Ever-Changing Standards: They change "the rules" so often you don't know how to please them or make them happy. They may not overtly tell you not to do something independent, or even encourage you to, but then they are critical of all attempts at you doing so.

○ *Someone Else - Past* | ○ *Someone Else - Current* | ○ *Me - Past* | ○ *Me - Current*

Substance Use: When they use substances often enough that their behavior is significantly altered regularly, you are at far more risk of abuse. Substances decrease our inhibitions to violent behavior. They may hide significant aspects of their usage as well.

○ *Someone Else - Past* | ○ *Someone Else - Current* | ○ *Me - Past* | ○ *Me - Current*

Breaking/Striking Things: Anything that demonstrates the physical violence that could happen to you. Punching walls, throwing objects, breaking possessions, beating on tables, etc.

○ *Someone Else - Past* | ○ *Someone Else - Current* | ○ *Me - Past* | ○ *Me - Current*

Physically Intimidating You/Blocking Your Movements: Things like standing in the way of doors so you can't exit, hovering over you when angry/upset.

○ *Someone Else - Past* | ○ *Someone Else - Current* | ○ *Me - Past* | ○ *Me - Current*

Threatens Violence: Things like "I'll kill you/myself if you leave me" or "I could knock you out right now." When called out on these threats, they will often say they were only kidding and/or would never really do it.

○ *Someone Else - Past* | ○ *Someone Else - Current* | ○ *Me - Past* | ○ *Me - Current*

Past Battering: You may hear from mutuals or past partners that the person was abusive in previous relationships. They say it's a lie, or their ex was "crazy," or it wasn't that bad, or the past partner deserved it.

○ *Someone Else - Past* | ○ *Someone Else - Current* | ○ *Me - Past* | ○ *Me - Current*

Coercive Control of Any Kind: Examples of this abound in my book *Unfuck Your Boundaries*; this could be financial control; control over your autonomy; tracking you; blocking you from other people; keeping you from having needs met (food, clothing, medicine, etc.); demeaning you privately; demeaning you in front of others; abusing your family, friends, kids, pets; "checking" on you at work or school; harassing you at work or school.

○ *Someone Else - Past* | ○ *Someone Else - Current* | ○ *Me - Past* | ○ *Me - Current*
Verbal Abuse of Any Kind: Critical, cruel, belittling, hurtful, degrading words aimed at you count as verbal abuse, as does calling you ugly names or cursing you out.

○ *Someone Else - Past* | ○ *Someone Else - Current* | ○ *Me - Past* | ○ *Me - Current*
Physical Force of Any Kind: They push you, shove you, hold you down, restrain you from leaving, etc.

Make any notes about patterns you noticed and changes you may need to make.

～Conclusion～

Ugh, okay. Stretch if you can, take the deepest breaths you can. That was a ton of work and you showed up for yourself and did some difficult work. If you feel a little (or a lottle) wrung out that makes utter sense. This is just me, a stranger from the pages of a book, telling you that I'm hella proud of your hard work. Just in case no one else has been on your team lately. Because even if that is true, and it is for a lot of people, you still deserve to heal. To have a more enriching life. To be a more complete human than your worst mistake. By being a better human one baby step at a time.

UNFUCKING ANGER: THE CHECK-IN

*B*ecoming skillful in the management of our emotions is not a recipe. If it was, we'd all follow the recipe and everyone would have a lovely homemade flan of a calm life. Instead, we have to test a lot of different stuff out and find what works best for us. It's tough work. Took a while to get fucked, takes awhile to get unfucked. Checking in on your progress is really helpful in not getting overwhelmed and dissuaded from continuing to work at it.

Are you finding yourself more or less activated by situations that would make you angry in the past? Are the differences in the level of anger or the number of instances of anger?

Are you finding that anger's grip on you is getting tighter or looser?

Are you finding that you have better skills to navigate your anger than you have in the past?

Do you believe that you have more control over your emotions that you have in the past?

Are certain skills becoming easier to access and utilize once you are activated? Do you see the potential for them becoming second nature?

Recommended Reading

Sacred Rest: Recover Your Life, Renew Your Energy, Restore Your Sanity by Dr. Saundra Dalton-Smith

Boundaries Conversations Deck by Dr. Faith G. Harper

How to Be Accountable: Take Responsibility to Change Your Behavior, Boundaries, and Relationships by Dr. Faith G. Harper and Joe Biel

How to Be Accountable Workbook: Take Responsibility to Change Your Behavior, Boundaries, and Relationships by Dr. Faith G. Harper and Joe Biel

Stress Coping Deck by Dr. Faith G. Harper

Unfuck Your Anger: Using Science to Understand Frustration, Rage, and Forgiveness by Dr. Faith G. Harper

Unfuck Your Boundaries: Build Better Relationships through Consent, Communication, and Expressing Your Needs by Dr. Faith G. Harper

Unfuck Your Boundaries Workbook: Build Better Relationships through Consent, Communication, and Expressing Your Needs by Dr. Faith G. Harper

Unfuck Your Stress: Using Science to Cope with Distress and Embrace Excitement by Dr. Faith G. Harper

All the Rage: Buddhist Wisdom on Anger and Acceptance edited by Andrea Miller and the Editors of the Shambhala Sun

Nonviolent Communication: A Language of Life by Marshall B. Rosenberg

Empowered Boundaries: Speaking Truth, Setting Boundaries, and Inspiring Social Change by Cristien Storm

Anger: Wisdom for Cooling the Flames by Thich Nhat Hanh

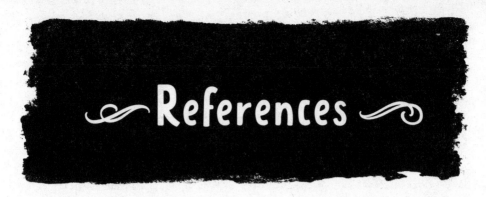

References

"Affect Regulation and Addictive Aspects of Repetitive Self-Injury in Hospitalized Adolescents." (2010, January 04). Retrieved from sciencedirect.com/science/article/abs/pii/S0890856709606390

Barrett-Lennard, G. (1997). "The Recovery of Empathy: Toward Others and Self." In Bohart, A. & Greenberg, L., *Empathy Reconsidered: New directions in Psychotherapy* (pp. 103–121). Washington, DC: American Psychological Association Press. doi:10.1037/10226-004.

Behavioral Tech, LLC (n.d.). What is DBT? | Behavioral Tech. behavioraltech.org/resources/whatisdbt.cfm

Besharat, Mohammad Ali; Nia, Mahin Etemadi; Farahani, Hojatollah. (2013). "Anger and Major Depressive Disorder: The Mediating Role of Emotion Regulation and Anger Rumination." *Asian Journal of Psychiatry*, 6, 35-41.

Carter, L., & Minirth, F. B. (1993). *The Anger Workbook*. Nashville, TN: Thomas Nelson.

"Childhood Origins of Self-Destructive Behavior." (1991). *American Journal of Psychiatry*, 148(12), 1665-1671. doi:10.1176/ajp.148.12.1665.

Harper, F. G. (2018). *This Is Your Brain on Depression*. Microcosm Publishing.

Harper, F. G. (2017). *Unfuck Your Brain: Using Science to Get over Anxiety, Depression, Anger, Freak-Outs, and Triggers*. Microcosm Publishing.

Heider, F. (1958) *The Psychology of Interpersonal Relations*, New York: Wiley.

James, M. (2017). *Ho'oponopono: Your Path to True Forgiveness*. Carlsbad, CA: Crescendo Publishing.

Jarrett-Kerr, N. (n.d.). "Six Steps to Discernment in Decision-Making." LinkedIn. linkedin.com/pulse/six-steps-discernment-decision-making-nick-jarrett-kerr

Jones, E. E. and Davis, K. E. (1965) "From Acts to Dispositions: The Attribution Process in Social Psychology," in L. Berkowitz (ed.), *Advances in Experimental Social*

Psychology (Volume 2, pp. 219-266), New York: Academic Press.

Jones, E. E. and Harris, V. A. (1967). "The Attribution of Attitudes." *Journal of Experimental Social Psychology*, 3, 1-24.

Jones, M.B., and Jones, D.R. (1995). "Preferred Pathways of Behavioural Contagion." *Journal of Psychiatric Research*, 29:193-209.

Jones, E. E. and Nisbett, R. E. (1972). "The Actor and the Observer: Divergent Perceptions of the Causes of the Behavior," in E. E. Jones, D. E. Kanouse, H. H. Kelley, R. E. Nisbett, S. Valins and B. Weiner (eds.), *Attribution: Perceiving the Causes of Behavior* (pp. 79-94). Morristown, NJ: General Learning Press.

Jordan, Judith. (1997). "Relational Development through Mutual Empathy." doi:10.1037/10226-015.

Leahy, R.L., Tirch, D., & Napolitano, L.A. (2011). *Emotion Regulation in Psychotherapy: A Practitioner's Guide, 1st Edition*. The Guilford Press, New York.

Lee, C., & Ghiya, S. (2012). "Influence of Alternate Nostril Breathing on Heart Rate Variability in Non-practitioners of Yogic Breathing." *International Journal of Yoga*, 5(1), 66. doi:10.4103/0973-6131.91717.

Lindebaum, D., & Geddes, D. (2015). "The Place and Role of (Moral) Anger in Organizational Behavior Studies." *Journal of Organizational Behavior*, 37(5), 738–757. doi:10.1002/job.2065.

Luskin, F. (2016). *Forgive for Good*. New York, NY: HarperOne.

Mohan, R., Jain (2015). *Trauma-Sensitive Yoga in Therapy: Bringing the Body into Treatment*. New York: W.W. Norton & Company.

Fava, M., & Rosenbaum, J. F. (1998). "Anger Attacks in Depression." *Depression and Anxiety*, 8(S1), 59-63. doi:10.1002/(sici)1520-6394(1998)8:1 3.0.co;2-y.

Fernandez, E., & Johnson, S. L. (2016). "Anger in Psychological Disorders: Prevalence, Presentation, Etiology and Prognostic Implications." *Clinical Psychology Review*, 46, 124–135. doi.org/10.1016/j.cpr.2016.04.012.

Gill, C. (2011a). "Relational-Centered Research for Psychotherapists: Exploring Meanings and Experience." *Counselling and Psychotherapy Research Journal*, 11(4), 326–327. doi.org/10.1080/14733145.2011.624838.

Goldstein, David S(Sep 2010) "Adrenaline and Noradrenaline," in: eLS. John Wiley & Sons Ltd., Chichester. els.net [doi: 10.1002/9780470015902.a0001401.pub2].

"Effect of Alternate Nostril Breathing on Cardiovascular Parameters in Obese Young Adults." *International Journal of Physiology*, 3(1), 108. doi:10.5958/2320-

608x.2015.00024.4.

Mohanty, S. (2016). Comments on "Alternate Nostril Breathing at Different Rates and Its Influence on Heart Rate Variability in Non Practitioners of Yoga." *Journal of Clinical and Diagnostic Research*. doi:10.7860/jcdr/2016/20276.8145.

Neff, K. D., & Dahm, K. A. (2015). "Self-Compassion: What It Is, What It Does, and How It Relates to Mindfulness," in *Handbook of Mindfulness and Self-Regulation* (pp. 121-137). Springer, New York, NY.

Patel, A. (2017, August 10). "When Anxiety Turns into Anger, Experts Say You Shouldn't Ignore It." Retrieved from: globalnews.ca/news/3654939/anxiety-and-anger/

Perry, J. C., & Cooper, S. H. (1986). "A Preliminary Report on Defenses and Conflicts Associated with Borderline Personality Disorder." *Journal of the American Psychoanalytic Association*, 34(4), 863-893. doi:10.1177/000306518603400405.

Pert, C. B., & Marriot, N. (2007). *Everything You Need to Know to Feel Good*. London: Hay House.

Plowden, Keith O.; Adams, Linda Thompson; Wiley, Dana. (2016). "Black and Blue: Depression and African American Men." Archives of *Psychiatric Nursing*, 30, 630-635.

Preidt, R. (n.d.). "Depression May Be Worse When Accompanied by Anger, Irritability," WebMD. Retrieved from webmd.com/depression/news/20130911/depression-may-be-worse-when-accompanied-by-anger-irritability

Rao U. DSM-5: "Disruptive Mood Dysregulation Disorder." *Asian Journal of Psychiatry*. 2014;11:119–123. doi:10.1016/j.ajp.2014.03.002.

Rosellini, G., & Worden, M. (1985). *Of Course You're Angry*. United States of America: Hazeldon.

Ross, L. (1977). "The Intuitive Psychologist and His Shortcomings: Distortions in the Attribution Process," in L. Berkowitz (ed.), *Advances in Experimental Social Psychology* (Volume 10, pp. 173-240), Orlando, FL: Academic Press.

Ross, L, Amabile, T. M. and Steinmetz, J. L.(1977). "Social Roles, Social Control and Biases in Social Perception," *Journal of Personality and Social Psychology*, 35, 485-494.

Ross, L., Lepper, M. R. and Hubbard, M. (1975). "Perseverance in Self-Perception and Social Perception: Biased Attributional Processes in the Debriefing Paradigm," *Journal of Personality and Social Psychology*, 32, 880-892.

Safer DJ. "Irritable Mood and the Diagnostic and Statistical Manual of Mental

Disorders. *Child Adolesc Psychiatry Ment Health*. 2009;3(1):35. Published 2009 Oct 24. doi:10.1186/1753-2000-3-35.

Sahu, A., Gupta, P., & Chatterjee, B. (2014). Depression is more than just sadness: A case of excessive anger and its management in depression. Indian Journal of Psychological Medicine, 36(1), 77. doi:10.4103/0253-7176.127259

Segal, Z.V., Williams, M., Teasdale, J.D., (2002). *Mindfulness-Based Cognitive Therapy for Depression: A New Approach to Preventing Relapse.* Guildford Publications, New York.

Self-injury (Cutting, Self-Harm or Self-Mutilation). (2016, August 17). Retrieved from mentalhealthamerica.net/self-injury

Singh, N. N., Lancioni, G. E., Singh, S. D., Winton, A. S. W., Sabaawi, M., Wahler, R. G., & Singh, J. (2007). "Adolescents with Conduct Disorder Can Be Mindful of Their Aggressive Behavior." *Journal of Emotional and Behavioral Disorders*, 15(1), 56-63.

Sussex Publishers. (n.d.-a). "Preventing Conflict through Self-Empathy." *Psychology Today.* psychologytoday.com/us/blog/empathic-intervision/202009/preventing-conflict-through-self-empathy

Sussex Publishers. (n.d.). "The Self in Empathy: Self-Empathy." *Psychology Today.* psychologytoday.com/us/blog/empathic-intervision/202007/the-self-in-empathy-self-empathy

Teasdale, J.D., Segal, Z.V., Williams, J.M.G., Ridgeway, V.A., Soulsby, J.M., Lau, M.A., 2000. "Prevention of Relapse/Recurrence in Major Depression by Mindfulness Based Cognitive Therapy." *Journal of Consulting and Clinical Psychology*, 68, 615–623.

Weisinger, H. (1985). *Dr. Weisinger's Anger Workout Book.* New York: Quill.

Whitlock, J.L., Exner-Cortens, D. & Purington, A. (under review). "Validity and Reliability of the Non-suicidal Self-Injury Assessment Test (NSSI-AT)."

ABOUT THE AUTHOR

Faith G. Harper, LPC-S, ACS, ACN, is a badass, funny lady with a PhD. She's a licensed professional counselor, board supervisor, certified sexologist, and applied clinical nutritionist with a private practice and consulting business in San Antonio, TX. She has been an adjunct professor and a TEDx presenter, and proudly identifies as a woman of color and uppity intersectional feminist. She is the author of dozens of books.

MORE BY DR. FAITH

Books

The Autism Partner Handbook (with Joe Biel and Elly Blue)
The Autism Relationships Handbook (with Joe Biel)
Befriend Your Brain
Coping Skills
How to Be Accountable (with Joe Biel)
This Is Your Brain on Depression
Unfuck Your Addiction
Unfuck Your Adulting
Unfuck Your Anger
Unfuck Your Anxiety
Unfuck Your Blow Jobs
Unfuck Your Body
Unfuck Your Boundaries
Unfuck Your Brain
Unfuck Your Cunnilingus
Unfuck Your Friendships
Unfuck Your Grief
Unfuck Your Intimacy
Unfuck Your Stress
Unfuck Your Worth
Unfuck Your Writing (with Joe Biel)
Woke Parenting (with Bonnie Scott)

Workbooks

Achieve Your Goals
The Autism Relationships Workbook (with Joe Biel)
How to Be Accountable Workbook (with Joe Biel)
Unfuck Your Anger Workbook
Unfuck Your Anxiety Workbook
Unfuck Your Body Workbook
Unfuck Your Boundaries Workbook
Unfuck Your Intimacy Workbook
Unfuck Your Worth Workbook
Unfuck Your Year

Zines

The Autism Handbook (with Joe Biel)
BDSM FAQ
Dating
Defriending
Detox Your Masculinity (with Aaron Sapp)
Emotional Freedom Technique
Getting Over It
How to Find a Therapist
How to Say No
Indigenous Noms
Relationshipping
The Revolution Won't Forget the Holidays
Self-Compassion
Sex Tools
Sexing Yourself
STI FAQ (with Aaron Sapp)
Surviving
This Is Your Brain on Addiction
This Is Your Brain on Grief
This Is Your Brain on PTSD
Unfuck Your Consent
Unfuck Your Forgiveness
Unfuck Your Mental Health Paradigm
Unfuck Your Sleep
Unfuck Your Work
Vision Boarding
Woke Parenting #1–6 (with Bonnie Scott)

Other

Boundaries Conversation Deck
Stress Coping Skills Deck
How Do You Feel Today? (poster)

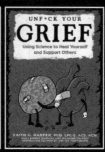
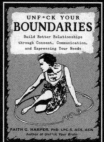

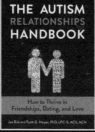
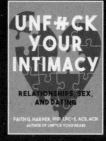

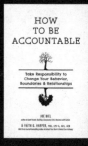